Pine N[barcode]

Basketry

for Beginners

Step-by-Step Guide to Beautiful Pine Needle
Basketry With Coiling, Stitching, and Design
Techniques Inspired by Nature

By Josh Bennett

Contents

Thank you for buying this book and I hope that you will find it useful. If you will want to share your thoughts on this book, you can do so by leaving a review on the Amazon page, it helps me out a lot.

Chapter 1: Introduction to Pine Needle Basketry

So, pine needle basketry isn't just some quaint pastime you stumble into when you're bored on a Sunday. We're talking about a craft with roots so deep, they probably have their own zip code in history. Think about it: before TikTok, before the internet, before people even thought about writing stuff down, there were already folks hunched over, threading pine needles into baskets. And this wasn't just in one little corner of the world, either. Nah, it's global. If you could spot a pine tree and you had hands, chances are you were making baskets—or at least knew someone who was.

Now, let's talk about why pine needles make such killer material for baskets. It's kind of wild when you think about it. These things are everywhere—falling all over the forest floor, getting stuck in your socks, making a mess in your backyard. But to our ancestors? Gold. If you treat the needles right—soak them, maybe chat them up a little—they'll bend and twist without snapping. Once they dry, though? Forget about it. You could probably use those baskets to fend off wild animals (okay, maybe not, but you get the idea). Tough stuff. And since pine trees aren't exactly endangered, you never had to worry about running short. Mother Nature was basically running an endless supply store, and the price was right: free.

But here's where things get spicy. In North America, especially in the southeast and southwest where you trip over pine trees just walking to the mailbox, Indigenous folks took this basketry game and dialed it up to eleven. For them, a basket wasn't just a place to drop your berries or lug around roots. Nah, these were the OG storybooks, the original family photo albums. Every coil, every stitch, every little decorative knot—they meant something. Some patterns were like secret handshakes, only people in the know could read them. And the colors? Sometimes made from berries, sometimes from clay, sometimes from who-knows-what, but always with purpose. These baskets got passed down like precious family secrets, showing up at weddings, ceremonies, and big gatherings. Some were used for everyday chores, but others? Basically sacred objects. Try making your Rubbermaid bin do that.

And the artistry! Some of these older baskets are so ridiculously intricate you start to question if they were made by wizards. We're talking patterns that reflect the stars, rivers, animals, even the struggles and joys of daily life. Skills like these don't just pop out of nowhere—they're the result of generations of practice, trial and error, and probably a few "oops, that's not how grandma did it" moments.

Let's not forget, though: coiled basketry is a worldwide phenomenon. People everywhere grabbed whatever was handy—reeds, grasses, bark, palm fronds—and started coiling away. But pine needle baskets have their own special vibe. There's something about the scent, the texture, the way the needles click together. It's like holding a little piece of the forest in your hands. And in those pine-heavy regions, the tradition wasn't just about practicality. It was about community, respect for the land, and making sure you never took more than what you needed. Kind of the original sustainability movement, if you think about it.

Flash forward to today, and you'd think something this old might be collecting dust in a museum somewhere. But nope—pine needle basketry is having a full-on renaissance. People are picking it up for all sorts of reasons. Some want to unplug from the endless scrolling and get their hands dirty (in a good way). Others are all about that slow, meditative process—you know, the kind of thing that makes you forget about your inbox for a few hours. Plus, there's a real sense of pride in making something by hand, especially when the end result is both drop-dead gorgeous and useful.

Modern makers aren't just copying the old ways, either. They're remixing everything—throwing in bold colors, wild shapes, even mixing pine needles with yarn, wire, or beads. You might see baskets that look like they came straight from a thousand years ago, sitting right next to ones that could be in a modern art gallery. The vibe is all about blending tradition and innovation, showing that this isn't just a relic—it's a living, breathing craft.

And let's be real, gifting someone a pine needle basket you made yourself? That's a flex. It's personal, it's unique, and it carries a story—way better than some store-bought mug. So whether you're in it for the zen, the art, or the sweet smell of pine, one thing's for sure: pine needle basketry isn't just surviving—it's thriving, evolving, and proving that sometimes the oldest crafts still have plenty of tricks up their sleeves.

Why Pine Needle Basketry Just Clicks for Beginners

Pine needle basketry is like the underdog of the craft world, and honestly, I wish more people knew about it. It's not just "beginner friendly" because it's cheap (though, yeah, your wallet stays happy). It's also about accessibility. Like, you don't need some Pinterest-perfect craft room or a background in fine arts. All you need is a little curiosity and, you know, some trees nearby. Even if you live in the suburbs or a city, there's probably a park somewhere with pines. Heck, raid your neighbor's yard if you have to—just don't get caught.

And don't even get me started on the whole "gathering supplies" process. Most crafts make you jump through hoops— tracking down rare yarn colors, hunting for specialty glues, spending hours reading reviews because, God forbid, you buy the wrong type of clay. With basketry, you're basically just out for a walk, picking up stuff nature literally threw at your feet. It's like a scavenger hunt, but you actually want what you find. The pine smell?

Seriously underrated. It's like being transported to a cabin in the mountains, minus the bugs and questionable plumbing.

Now, when it comes to the actual making, it's shockingly intuitive. Like, you might look up a YouTube video or two, but after the first couple of awkward coils, your hands just get it. It's one of those crafts where the process is almost meditative. You're looping, you're stitching, you zone out, and suddenly you've got a basket forming in your lap. Sometimes I lose track of time and realize I've been sitting there for hours, just vibing. No stress, no deadlines—just you and your little pine needle pile.

And let's talk about the "imperfection is cool" thing. A lot of crafts have this pressure for everything to be Instagram-level flawless, but pine needle baskets? Nah. Wonky stitches? Adds flavor. Uneven coils? That's called "texture," my friend. It's the kind of project where mistakes aren't just tolerated—they're straight-up celebrated. Each basket turns out different, with its own personality. You can crank out a tiny coaster just to feel productive, or go all-in and make a giant bread basket that looks like it came from some rustic farmhouse kitchen. Either way, you get to stand back, look at it, and think, "Yep, made that with my own two hands."

Honestly, I think part of the magic is how this craft sneaks up on you. You go in expecting to just kill some time, but next thing you know, you're looking at everyday stuff differently. Fallen needles? Craft supplies. That old thread you never used up? Might as well give it a second life. It sort of shifts your mindset—suddenly you're seeing raw potential everywhere.

Oh, and the eco-friendly angle? Let's be real, half the "sustainable" crafts out there still have you buying a bunch of new stuff. Pine needle basketry is the real deal. You're literally cleaning up the yard and making something useful. No waste, no extra junk, just pure upcycling. You could even call it "forest-to-table," if baskets were food—just don't eat them, obviously.

And, look, there's something quietly powerful about creating with what you've got. No gatekeeping, no fancy prerequisites. It's just you, nature's leftovers, and a bit of patience. You end up with something practical (seriously, these baskets hold up), and it feels good—like, deep-down, "I made this" good. You want a craft that's relaxing, rewarding, smells great, and earns you eco points? Pine needle basketry checks every box, then builds a box to put your stuff in.

So yeah, if you're bored, broke, stressed, or just want to brag about your earthy, artsy side—grab some needles and get coiling. Trust me, your future self (and maybe your coffee table) will thank you.

The Basic Principles of Coiled Basketry

Alright, let's just get into it and unpack the wild, weird world of coiled basketry—specifically pine needle baskets, which, honestly, are way cooler than they sound. You ever see one in a thrift store and think, "Who actually makes these?" Guess what, it could be you, and you don't even need to be some ancient craft guru or whatever.

So, coiling. It's the low-drama cousin of weaving. No wrestling with a loom or getting your fingers in knots. It's literally just wrapping and stitching, and somehow, it ends up looking like you know what you're doing, even if you're watching reality TV in the background. I swear, it's almost like therapy without the copay.

Step one: pine needles. Not the scraggly, short ones that poke holes in your socks, but those long, flexible ones. Think of them as nature's spaghetti—only way less edible. You grab a handful, bunch them up, and roll them into a burrito shape. You can tie a knot at the end to keep things from unraveling, or, if you wanna look extra pro, start with a little wooden disc or button. It's basically the crafting equivalent of using training wheels, and there's no shame in it.

Now, the stitching. This is where you get into a kind of meditative groove. You just grab some thread—raffia, sinew, embroidery floss, whatever's handy—and start sewing your bundle into a spiral. Every stitch hooks the new layer onto the one before it, so your basket doesn't just explode in your face (which, believe me, is as fun as it sounds). You can keep it flat for a tray, or start angling the coils to build up some sides. Wanna get avant-garde? Make a basket with a wavy rim, or a weird sculpture that looks like it crawled out of a Dr. Seuss book.

The magic with pine needles is how bendy they are. You can coax them into all sorts of shapes. Hard corners, big curves, wild zig-zags—whatever your caffeine-fueled brain dreams up. I've seen people use them to make hats, jewelry, wall hangings, and even little animal figures. Basically, if you can imagine it, there's probably someone out there who's tried it with pine needles and lived to tell the tale.

Let's talk stitching for a sec. The basic straight stitch is Basketry For Dummies level. Needle through the last coil, wrap around the new bundle, repeat. You don't even have to be careful, honestly. If you mess up, no one will know except you— and maybe your cat, who's probably judging you anyway. When that gets boring (because it will, eventually), there's a whole world of fancier stitches. You've got the V-stitch, which looks all geometric and trendy, or the wheat stitch, which basically says, "Yeah, I know what I'm doing." Add in some colored thread or beads, and suddenly people are asking where you bought your "artisan" basket.

What's wild is how forgiving this craft is. You make a mistake? Just stitch over it. Basket looking a little wonky? Call it "organic." Want to stop halfway and make a donut-shaped thing? Go ahead, invent a new trend. There's this freedom in coiling that you don't get with other crafts. No pattern police are coming for you. It's all about playing, experimenting, and getting your hands a little dirty.

And, look, pine needle baskets aren't just pretty—they've got some history, too. Native American tribes have been making these for ages, passing the skill down for generations. It's kind of wild to think about how you, chilling in your living room with laptop crumbs on your shirt, are carrying on this ancient tradition. There's something a little magical about that, honestly.

You don't even need fancy supplies to get started. Pine needles? Free, if you've got a tree nearby (bonus points for foraging vibes). Thread? Whatever's lying around. Needle? Any sharp thing that pokes a hole. It's a craft you can do on a shoestring budget while still flexing some serious creative muscle. Plus, your hands will smell like Christmas trees, which is a weirdly nice bonus.

So yeah, coiled basketry is where it's at if you want something hands-on, chill, and totally customizable. You can make practical stuff—like trays for your keys and loose change—or just let loose and create something totally off-the-wall. And at the end of the day, you get to look at this thing you made out of literal yard waste and think, "Dang, I did that." Way more satisfying than scrolling social media until your eyeballs hurt.

Bottom line? Coiled basketry is stupid simple to start, low-key addictive, and way more forgiving than you'd expect. All you need is a pile of pine needles, a needle, some thread, and a little patience. Go on, give it a shot—worst case, you end up with a lumpy basket and a good story. Best case, you unlock a new obsession and start making baskets for everyone you know (whether they want one or not).

The Journey Ahead

So you wanna get into pine needle basketry, huh? Alright, let's really get into it—no holding back. This isn't just a weekend craft you pick up, get bored with, and forget behind the couch with your half-finished macramé plant hanger. Nope. This is hands-on, earthy, and a little bit wild. Imagine you, boots crunching through pine needles, pockets stuffed full of those long, sappy beauties, and a whole new set of calluses on your fingers. Welcome to the club.

If you've never done anything like this before, trust me, that's actually a good thing. You're not weighed down by "rules" or someone else's idea of what a basket should look like. You get to make all the weird mistakes and happy accidents that lead to something totally original. Plus, you know, you get bragging rights for making stuff out of literal yard trash. Honestly, if anyone gives you a side-eye for collecting pine needles, just tell them you're an artist. Works every time.

Let's talk about getting started. Finding the right needles is basically a scavenger hunt for grownups. The long ones are the golden ticket—think ponderosa, longleaf, or whatever your local trees are throwing down. If it smells like Christmas and snaps less than a breadstick, you're in business. You'll learn pretty quickly that prepping them is a non-negotiable step. Skip it and you're in snap city, fighting with every coil. So, yeah, soak those needles, get 'em pliable, and embrace the sticky fingers. It just comes with the territory.

Now, coiling and stitching? That's where things get spicy. At first, it's gonna feel like wrestling a slippery snake and a ball of yarn at the same time. Your hands will cramp. You might curse a little. (Or a lot. No judgment.) But then—honestly, it's kind of magic—your hands start to get the rhythm. It goes from "what the heck am I doing" to "hey, that's a basket!" in like, three episodes of your favorite podcast. That first time the shape holds together and you realize you didn't totally botch it? Chef's kiss. Top-tier dopamine hit.

And don't even get me started on the possibilities. There's literally no end to what you can do with this. Classic round baskets? Sure. Wild, lumpy, free-form creations that look like something a woodland elf would haul around? Absolutely. Wanna throw in some random yarn, leftover beads, feathers you found on a walk? Go for it. You're not just stuck with brown and green either—grab some dye, go nuts. Make it neon pink if you want. If anyone tells you it's "not traditional," just smile and keep weaving. Tradition's great and all, but so is having fun and making something that screams you.

Oh, and let's be real: you're gonna mess up. Everyone does. Your first basket might look like it survived a tumble down the stairs. But every little wobble and wonky stitch is part of your story. Think of it like tattoos for your craft—each weird curve is a memory. You'll get better without even realizing it. One day you'll look back at your first funky creation and laugh, but you'll also have a weird affection for it. It's proof you started something new, and didn't let being a total newbie stop you.

Pine needle basketry is basically the original fidget spinner. It calms the nerves, keeps your hands busy, and gives you an excuse to ignore your phone for a few hours. Plus, it's sort of meditative—there's something about the repetitive motion, the smell of pine, the feel of natural materials in your hands that just grounds you. And when you finally finish? You've got a piece of art, a container, and a story, all rolled into one.

But here's the deeper bit nobody tells you: when you sit down with a pile of needles and start weaving, you're tapping into something old. Like, ancient old. People have been making baskets out of whatever nature gave them for ages—way before craft stores were a thing. You're carrying on this quiet conversation with the past, adding your own twist to it. And maybe someday, someone will pick up your basket, turn it over in their hands, and wonder about the person who made it. Boom—instant legacy.

So, don't overthink it. Grab what you've got, get a little messy, and just start. Make the ugliest, weirdest, most "what even is that" basket you can imagine. Then make another one. And another. Before you know it, you'll have a whole stack of them, each one better than the last, each one with its own little quirks and stories. You'll be the person who can turn pine needles—literal yard waste—into something beautiful, useful, and totally unique. Kinda cool, right? Now get out there and start weaving. The trees are waiting.

Chapter 2: Gathering and Preparing Pine Needles

Finding and Identifying the Right Pine Needles

Alright, let's get real about pine needles—because if you're gonna make a basket worth bragging about, it all starts way before you ever pick up a needle or thread. Forget the Pinterest-perfect craft room for a minute. Nope, your first move is actually heading out into the wild, or at least somewhere with enough trees to make a squirrel jealous.

Picture it: you're wandering through a forest, maybe even just your neighborhood park, dodging the occasional dog walker and hoping you don't step on something questionable. Pine needles are everywhere, right? Well, not all of 'em are basket-worthy. If you want your basket to look legit (and not like a kindergarten project), you need needles that are long and bendy—seriously, the longer and more flexible, the better. Short, brittle needles? Pass. They'll snap, make your basket lumpy, and basically just ruin your day.

If you're in the U.S., you're in luck. The longleaf pine is basically the holy grail— those needles can get wild, sometimes up to a foot and a half long, which is just ridiculous in the best way. Slash pine and ponderosa? Also solid choices. Basically, if you see a tree dropping needles that look like they could double as spaghetti, grab 'em.

Now, collecting these babies is kind of zen. You're not yanking them off branches like a maniac (don't be that person). You're looking down, scanning the ground for clusters of brown, mature needles that have already fallen. The green ones might look shiny and fresh, but trust me, they're a sticky disaster. Sticky sap everywhere, ruining your tools and probably your mood. Plus, green needles can mess up the color and even get moldy when you try to weave them in. Gross.

So yeah, stick to the brown, fully dried-out needles. They're flexible but not floppy, and they won't gum up your hands. Plus, that natural earthy color? Chef's kiss. Your basket will look like you actually know what you're doing, even if you're just winging it.

Let's get real—finding pine trees is just the beginning. If you're serious about making baskets, you have to channel your inner nature sleuth. You gotta pay attention, notice where these trees are actually thriving. It's wild how much the dirt under your feet matters. Pines that dig in and survive on sandy or rocky patches, where life's a bit tougher? Those guys crank out needles like little bodybuilders—firm, tough, and they don't flop around when you start coiling. It's like, "Yeah, I survived that drought, here's a needle you can actually use." On the flip side, you ever try needles from a tree growing in a soggy, gloomy spot? Total disappointment—thin, snap-prone, sometimes moldy. Not what you want for a basket that's supposed to last.

And here's the thing: you've gotta experiment. Seriously, you'll end up with a pile of duds at first, and that's just part of the deal. Two trees, same species, side by side? The needles can be totally different. After a few rounds, though, you'll know which trees are the MVPs. Once you've scoped out a killer spot, guard it like it's a secret fishing hole—keep coming back when the season's right and you'll have prime material year after year. This whole process, honestly, it's more than just scavenging supplies—it turns into this almost meditative ritual. You start noticing stuff—how the trees shed, how the light hits certain patches, which spots have the best needles. Before you know it, you're not just making baskets, you're basically a pine whisperer, and every basket you finish feels like it's got a little piece of that place woven in.

Now, let's talk about not being a jerk to the forest. Ethical gathering isn't just a nice-to-have—it's non-negotiable. You only pick up what the trees are done with, period. Don't even think about yanking fresh needles off a branch, no matter how tempting that bright green looks. You might as well slap the tree in the face. Ripping off needles stresses the tree out, messes with its growth, opens it up to bugs—just don't. Only pick up what's already fallen. And, look, the forest floor isn't your personal craft store, alright? Those fallen needles are doing real work: protecting baby plants, keeping the dirt from washing away, feeding the soil as they break down. Take just what you need, leave the rest, and the forest keeps doing its thing. It's not just about being eco-friendly—there's something almost sacred about it. Treat the materials like a gift, not a right. That's how you keep the tradition going—by actually respecting where it all comes from. Every time you gather with care, you're adding a little more meaning to every basket you make.

Cleaning and Sorting the Needles

So here's the deal: cleaning and sorting pine needles isn't just something you do because some YouTube basket weaver said so. Nah. This step is like setting the stage for your entire project. Honestly, it's make-or-break territory. You rush through this? Your basket's gonna show it—like, every lumpy, dirty, sad bit will be there, haunting you. But if you take your time? Suddenly you're making something you actually wanna show people, not just your cat.

Digging into that first part—gathering pine needles off the forest floor. Sounds romantic, right? Nature, birds chirping, sun through the trees. Reality check: you're basically foraging through a crunchy carpet of old leaves, sticks, maybe the occasional squirrel glaring at you for stealing its stash. And those pine needles? They're a mixed bag. Some are long and lovely, others are bent, broken, or so caked in mud you wonder if they're even worth saving. Honestly, you develop an eye for the good ones after a while, but at first, you'll probably grab a bunch of junk. It's all part of the learning curve.

Anyway, once you've got your pile, the "shake 'em out" step is weirdly satisfying. I mean, you never really realize how much junk a handful of pine needles can hold until you start flinging it everywhere. Sometimes you'll even find a tiny beetle or a weird little pod stuck in there. And if you're shaking them out inside? Good luck explaining to your roommate why there's a mysterious pile of forest debris in the kitchen. Pro tip: do this outside unless you want your place smelling like mulch.

Now, onto the water part. Swishing those needles around is like giving them a spa day. The water turns all murky, which is kinda gross but also proof you're actually cleaning something, right? And there's something meditative about it—your hands in warm water, watching the grime float away. If you're the type who finds cleaning oddly calming, you'll probably dig this part. Just don't forget to rinse a couple times, or else you'll end up with needles that smell like wet dog and Palmolive. Not the vibe.

If you ever get a stubborn batch—ones that are sticky with sap or just seem extra nasty—don't be afraid to let them soak a bit longer, or use a few drops of dish soap. Seriously, a little goes a long way. Too much and you'll be rinsing forever, and if you leave any soap behind, your basket will hold onto that weird chemical scent like a grudge. Been there, regretted that.

Drying them is a lesson in patience. You might be tempted to speed things along with a hair dryer or by sticking them in the sun, but slow and steady wins here. Rushing means brittle needles, and brittle needles snap when you're weaving, basically turning your project into a rage-inducing puzzle. Plus, mildew? That's a whole new level of gross—nothing says "homemade" like a basket that smells like a forgotten gym sock.

Now we get to sorting. This is where you really get up close and personal with your needles. You'll notice every flaw, every weird twist, every speck of leftover dirt. It's kinda like speed-dating for pine needles— if they don't pass the vibe check, out they go. That papery sheath at the end? Just get rid of it. It doesn't look good, doesn't weave well, just… bye.

And don't sleep on organizing by length and straightness. The long, straight ones are your MVPs—they make the structure strong and pretty. The short, crooked, or weirdly chunky needles? They're not totally useless, though. Sometimes you need those oddballs to fill in weird gaps or start your basket without wasting the good stuff. It's like assembling a team—you need a few weirdos to make it all work.

One more thing: the more you handle your needles while sorting, the more you get a feel for the flexible, healthy ones. They should bend without snapping, almost like they're made for this (which, I guess, they kinda are). If you start to notice any that feel brittle, toss 'em. They'll betray you in the middle of a coil and ruin your day.

Bottom line? This whole cleaning and sorting thing is where you set yourself up for success. It's not glamorous, and it's definitely not quick, but it's absolutely worth it. Do it right, and weaving becomes this almost zen experience. Do it wrong, and you're just fighting with dirty, broken needles for hours. Your future self will thank you. Or curse you. Your call.

And that's basically it—clean, dry, sort, and you're ready to start weaving like a pro.

First off, if you're paying attention at this part, you can't help but notice the colors in those pine needles. Seriously, look close. Some are this buttery golden brown, like they just spent the summer at the beach, others go full-on redhead or give off these quiet, moody gray vibes. Forget about trying to make them all match—those color differences are where the magic's at. The pros? They lean in, using those natural shades to make the basket pop with stripes, patterns, or just a gentle fade that makes the whole thing feel alive. Of course, if you're one of those "everything must match" types, you could always dye them later, after you've cleaned them up. But for now, just focus on getting a big pile of neat, clean, ready-to-go needles. That's job number one.

I'm not gonna lie—this whole cleaning and sorting deal? It takes ages. It's not glamorous. But it's weirdly zen. You end up alone with your thoughts, picking through the needles, feeling the textures, trimming the scraggly bits. You start to get a sense for what each one could become—maybe this twisty one's gonna be the star of the rim, or that super straight one will anchor a strong row. A lot of basket makers admit this is their favorite part. It's quiet, it's slow, and it's the moment you really get to know your material. Almost meditative, honestly. It's like the pre-game ritual before the big creative burst.

Softening and Conditioning the Needles

Now, about those needles. If you're working with dried ones (which, trust me, you want to be—fresh needles are a sticky nightmare), you're in for a whole new headache: brittleness. They snap, they splinter, and suddenly you're inventing new curse words. Dry needles just don't want to bend; they'd rather break. And that's not gonna work for a nice, snug basket.

So you gotta soften those babies up. Most people just toss them in a bowl of warm water—nothing fancy, just enough to cover them. Give it half an hour, maybe an hour. The water sneaks into the fibers, bringing them back to life so they'll flex instead of snap. If your needles are old or just stubborn as hell, you can boil them for a minute or two, but you gotta watch them close. Leave them in too long and you end up with limp, sad noodles instead of basket material. Nobody wants that.

There's another trick, too—steaming. Grab a colander, hold your bundle over a pot of boiling water, and let the steam do its thing. Or, if you're feeling fancy, a garment steamer works great. Steaming's nice because you don't soak the needles all the way through, so they're ready to use a lot faster, and you don't have to worry about mold if you forget about them for a day.

So yeah, a little prep goes a long way. Get your needles soft, and your fingers will thank you later. Trust me.

Once you've softened the needles— soaked 'em or steamed 'em, whatever floats your boat—you can't just toss them aside and expect them to stay all bendy and lovely. Nope. Keep them wrapped up in something damp, like a towel or cloth. Not sopping wet, just... you know, moist enough. Otherwise, you'll come back and they'll be all brittle again, snapping like overcooked spaghetti before you even get started. Honestly, I just leave mine like that for hours, sometimes overnight if I forget (which, let's be real, happens a lot).

If you want to get a little fancy—and trust me, you do—grab a rag, dab it with a bit of olive oil or beeswax polish, and give those needles a quick rubdown. Total gamechanger. Not only do they end up with this gorgeous, earthy shine (they practically glow), but the oil helps lock in the moisture and keeps the fibers from splitting or going all haywire while you're coiling and stitching. It's not strictly required, but if you skip it? You're missing out on both the "oooh, pretty" factor and some serious durability. Plus, it just feels better in your hands. Smoother, you know?

Now, don't go overboard with the water. Needles that are soaked to the bone? They'll shrink when they finally dry in your basket, which means your careful stitches get loose and the whole thing ends up kinda floppy and sad. On the flip side, if you don't soften them enough, they'll crack and splinter, and you'll probably curse and toss half your stash. It takes a little practice to nail that sweet spot—supple but still with some backbone. You want 'em to bend easily but not just flop around.

Honestly, getting this right is way more important than it sounds. It's not just a checklist step—it sets the stage for everything that comes after. Mess this up and your basket's doomed before you even start weaving. Get it right, though, and you're golden. The needles work with you, not against you, and your finished basket ends up looking tight, shiny, and sturdy enough to survive a tumble off the table.

Building a Ready Supply

Here's something people don't talk about enough: half the magic of pine needle basketry is the whole ritual of hunting for your materials. You end up paying attention to the woods in a way most folks never do. You start to notice which trees drop the best needles, which patches of forest have the real bounty, and how the seasons shift everything. It's kinda meditative, and honestly, it just makes you feel more connected to the place you live.

The best time to go foraging? Late fall through winter, hands down. That's when the trees shed their old needles in thick carpets. You stroll through, and it's like nature just rolled out the red carpet for basket makers. If you plan your gathering trips around these times, you'll get way better results and won't be tempted to yank stuff off living trees (don't be that person). Plus, you'll end up with a stash that'll last you year-round, so you're never stuck waiting for the next drop.

Once you get into the groove, you'll want to keep a little stockpile going—nothing crazy, just enough so you're not scrambling. Clean 'em, pre-condition if you're on top of things, and keep them somewhere dry and safe. That way, whenever the urge to weave hits—rain, snow, or blazing summer—you're good to go. And honestly? There's something super satisfying about having your own hand-picked, ready-to-roll needles waiting for your next burst of creativity.

Storing pine needles is one of those things that sounds simple, but if you mess it up, you're gonna regret it. After you've collected and cleaned them (yeah, that's the boring part), you want to bundle the needles kinda loosely. Not tight—just enough so air can move around, or else you're basically asking for a mold party. Trust me, you don't want that. Toss those bundles into something that breathes: paper bags, old-school baskets, maybe a cloth sack (think cotton or linen, not your grandma's plastic Tupperware).

Airtight containers are a big nope—trapped moisture is sneaky and will turn your stash into a science experiment gone wrong before you know it. Keep your pine needle hoard somewhere cool and dry. Closet, spare shelf in the pantry, or a basement with a bit of airflow? All solid choices. Oh, and sunlight? Not your friend here. Leave your bundles cooking in the sun and you'll end up with brittle, faded needles that snap like old spaghetti. If you got fancy and misted the needles or rubbed in a little oil for flexibility, make sure they're dry as a bone before you store them for good, or you'll be dealing with fungus. Yuck.

Honestly, having a little stockpile of pine needles is a total game-changer. No more running out with a garbage bag every time you get a crafty itch. You can just grab what you need and get going, no drama. Plus, when you've got options, you can be picky. Want those long, beefy needles for a big basket? No problem. Need something fine and delicate for a little accent? You've got that too. After a while, your stash starts to look like an artist's paintbox—different colors, textures, even scents. Each bundle's got its own vibe, just waiting to be turned into something cool.

Now, don't be fooled—this early stage, the gathering and prepping, it's not just busywork. It's the backbone of the whole pine needle basket thing. If you skip it or half-ass it, you'll pay for it later, I promise.

Needles that are clean, sort of soft, and sorted by size are way easier to work with. You'll get tighter coils, smoother stitches, and your baskets will actually look like you know what you're doing. Plus, prepping the right way just makes the whole process less annoying and a lot more fun. Putting in that effort up front? That's how you end up with baskets you're actually proud to show off—not to mention, you're giving a little nod to the folks who've been doing this forever. Bottom line: if you respect your materials and put in the prep work, you set yourself up for a way better, way more satisfying ride. And hey, your finished baskets will show it.

Chapter 3: Tools and Materials You Will Need

So, you want to make a pine needle basket? Sweet. This is one of those old-school crafts that doesn't ask much from your wallet or your storage space. Honestly, half the fun is realizing how little gear you really need—no fancy machinery, no endless shopping lists. Just you, some needles, and a few odds and ends you probably already have kicking around the house.

Let's talk needles. Not the tiny, finger-stabbing kind for sewing buttons—nah, you want something beefy. Pine needles aren't exactly delicate, so your needle better be up for the job. Look for a big ol' tapestry needle, a chunky darning needle, or one of those blunt upholstery guys. You want an eye wide enough to jam some thick thread or raffia through—none of that dainty stuff. Honestly, the blunt tip is a lifesaver; it glides right through the coils without shredding your pine needles to bits. Trust me, you don't want to snap or fray those needles—nothing ruins your vibe faster. Beginners can totally stick with a straight needle, but once you're knee-deep in complex shapes or wrestling with tight corners, a curved needle might just save your sanity.

Now, here's the unsung hero nobody talks about: the awl. Yeah, it sounds like a pirate curse, but it's basically a pointy stick with a handle, and it'll change your life. Poke it between your basket coils to make space for your needle—no wrestling, no swearing (okay, maybe less swearing). You don't need anything fancy—borrow a metal skewer, a fat knitting needle, or even a chopstick you sharpened on a whim. Just make sure it's not rough, or you'll snag everything and cry. Once you start making tighter, fancier baskets, you'll wonder how you ever lived without a real awl.

When it comes to scissors don't overthink it, but don't use the kitchen junk drawer special either. You'll be trimming pine needles, chopping thread, and tidying up your basket's edges. Grab some sharp craft scissors or embroidery snips—if you're dealing with monster-sized needles, maybe even small garden shears. Sharpness is everything. Dull scissors are basically a crime against basketry. You want crisp cuts, not shredded ends that look like you let your dog at them.

Bottom line: you don't need a ton of stuff, but the right tools make this whole basket-weaving adventure a lot less headache-inducing. And hey, half the gear can be scavenged from around the house—bonus points for resourcefulness, right?

So here's the deal: You don't technically need a gauge to start making pine needle baskets—like, it's not life-or-death the way a needle or scissors are. But let's be real, especially if you're just dipping your toes in, that little gadget is a lifesaver for keeping things even. A gauge is basically a fancy name for something super simple: it could be a bit of plastic straw, a slice of copper pipe, or even some random rubber tubing you chopped to the right width. You just shove your pine needles through this thing while you're working, and boom—your coils come out the same thickness, not all wonky and lumpy. It's like training wheels for your hands. Yeah, if you're a total basket-whisperer, you can probably eyeball it and nail the uniformity. But for most of us? The gauge keeps things tight, tidy, and actually looking like you meant to make a basket, not a porcupine nest. Plus, once you get the hang of it and your fingers develop that sixth sense, you might toss the gauge aside anyway. Still, for anyone starting out, it's stupidly helpful. Trust me.

So, with just a few basic tools—a fat, blunt needle, a sharp awl, trusty scissors, and maybe a coil gauge for backup—you're pretty much set. No high-tech nonsense, just the essentials. That's the whole charm of this craft, honestly. It's all about the materials, your hands, and letting the pine needles shine. No distraction, no fuss—just the good stuff.

Threads, Bindings, and Stitching Materials

Here's where things get spicy—because let's face it, the thread or whatever you use to stitch everything together is just as important as the pine needles themselves. Sometimes, I'd even say it matters more. Pick the right binding material and suddenly your basket goes from "meh" to "damn, look at that!" This stuff isn't just holding the basket together; it's the backbone. Structure, color, vibe—all of it rides on what you choose to wrap those coils with.

Back in the day, people just grabbed whatever they could find nearby. We're talking raffia, split reeds, or if you want to go full hunter-gatherer, actual sinew yanked from animal tendons. Hardcore, right? It wasn't just about survival—it was about knowing what worked and what looked good. There's something kind of poetic about that, honestly.

Fast-forward to now, and the world's your oyster. You can stick with classic natural fibers or go rogue with synthetics. Every choice has its own pros and cons—some are tough as nails, some are all about the looks, some will make you want to pull your hair out because they tangle if you blink.

Raffia, though? Still a crowd-pleaser. It's got this earthy, laid-back look and is ridiculously easy to work with. It comes from the Raphia palm—mostly from Madagascar, fun fact—and you'll usually see it in a warm tan, but you can get it dyed in every color under the sun if you want to go wild. It's flexible, threads like a dream, and just sort of melts around the coils in a way that feels… right. The texture's nice, too—not too slippery, not too rough. Perfect for a basket you want to actually touch. Only thing is, raffia's not the Hulk—it won't hold up to years of rough-and-tumble use. So, yeah, go for it if you want something pretty or decorative, but maybe skip it if you're planning to haul bricks in your basket.

Bottom line: the thread or binding you pick sets the whole tone, so don't just grab the first thing you see. Play around, experiment, and find what clicks. That's half the fun, anyway.

If you want a basket that'll actually survive more than a week of use, waxed linen thread is a total game-changer. People rave about this stuff, and honestly, for good reason. It's crazy strong—like, you could probably tow a small dog with it (don't do that). The secret sauce? That wax coating. It doesn't just keep the thread from splitting into a million annoying fibers while you work, it also makes the stitches stick just a little, so everything holds together nice and snug. Plus, the wax gives you a bit of water resistance, which is great if your basket ends up in the wild (or, you know, on a kitchen counter somewhere).

Oh, and the colors? You've got options, trust me. Whether you're into subtle earth tones or want your basket to scream neon from across the room, you'll find a shade.

If you're the kind of person who wants their baskets to outlive their houseplants, waxed linen thread is basically the gold standard—it's reliable, looks polished, and just works.

Now, sinew's got a whole story of its own. Picture ancient folks, meticulously scraping tendons from their dinner to make binding for baskets. Hardcore, right? Real sinew is still around for the purists, but let's be real: most people these days reach for the synthetic stuff. Modern sinew's basically a high-tech upgrade—same strength, same flexibility, none of the mess (or ethical squeamishness). It usually comes as a flat strand, a bit waxy, and you can split it into thinner pieces if you want to get fancy with your stitching. The result? That super clean, tight look you see in traditional Native American pine needle baskets. Precision is the name of the game here.

But hey, why stop at the classics? Basketry's having a moment, and folks are getting wild with materials. Embroidery floss? Sure, it's not the toughest, but the color options are endless and the shine is gorgeous for tiny, detailed work. Cotton cord steps up with a chunkier, softer vibe—think cozy, laid-back baskets. And don't even get me started on leather strips. They're a pain to work with (seriously, punch holes first or your hands will hate you), but the end result is this rich, rustic feel that's hard to beat.

At the end of the day, picking your binding material is basically like choosing your fighter in a video game. You want something tough enough to hold everything together, flexible enough so you're not wrestling with it every five seconds, and—most important—something that fits your style. Because, let's be honest, half the fun is making something that actually looks cool sitting on your table.

Optional Accessories and Enhancements

Alright, let's get real about pine needle basketry. Yeah, you can totally start out with just some needles and a few basic tools—nothing wrong with keeping it simple. But, if you're looking to flex those creative muscles, there's a whole rabbit hole of optional add-ons and shiny extras that can take your baskets from "quaint" to "whoa, did you make that?"

First up, let's talk bling. Beads, little gemstones, shells—these aren't just random decorations you slap on at the end. Nah, serious basket makers stitch these right into the coils as they go, so the whole thing just flows together. You could thread in some tiny glass beads and get these glimmering, light-catching lines running through your basket. Or maybe you bury a chunk of abalone shell in there—bam, instant conversation piece. And it's not just about looking pretty. These touches make each basket weirdly personal, almost like you're sneaking in a hidden message or a piece of your own story. Some folks even pick embellishments that mean something in their culture or hometown, so the basket ends up carrying more history than your average family heirloom. Seriously, a well-placed bead or shell turns a pine needle bowl into a mini time capsule.

Now, about that center bit—sometimes called the medallion or base. This is like the basket's heart and soul. Some people go with a polished chunk of walnut or a carved disk of bone, others get wild with pottery or even flashy glass. It's not just for looks, though it totally catches the eye and gives your basket some instant swagger. Starting with a solid center also makes the first few coils way easier (especially if you're new and still figuring out how not to have your basket look like a lopsided pancake). No shame in letting the center do some heavy lifting.

And then, color. Pine needles are great in their earthy, natural shades, but maybe you're not feeling the whole "forest elf" vibe. This is where dyes come in—natural plant dyes or modern chemical ones, you do you. People have been dunking needles in onion skins, madder root, indigo, all that jazz, for centuries. Some folks dye just a few needles for cool patterns, others go full-on rainbow. Not gonna lie: dyeing takes patience, unless you want to end up with blotchy, sad-looking needles. But when it works? You get these crazy gradients and custom color pops that make your basket stand out from the crowd.

So, yeah, you can keep it basic. But honestly, why not throw in some extras? It turns a simple craft into something that's got style, history, and a good dose of your own personality. And isn't that kind of the point?

You wouldn't think keeping pine needles soft would be such a big deal, right? But, honestly, it's kind of everything if you want your basket-making to go smoothly and not end with you swearing at a pile of snapped twigs. Most seasoned basket folks keep a spray bottle handy—just a quick spritz here and there keeps the needles from drying out and turning into brittle little nightmares, especially when the air's dry. If you start coiling and stitching with dry needles, good luck. They'll crack faster than you can say "ruined project." A damp cloth works too—just wrap your working bundle up, and you don't have to keep running to the sink every ten minutes. Little things like this—keeping your needles happy—save your hands and your sanity, and honestly, they make the whole process way more enjoyable.

Now, you don't need a bunch of fancy extras to make a basket that holds together, but having a few tricks up your sleeve really shows off what pine needle basketry can do. Toss in some thoughtful tools or techniques and suddenly you're not just making baskets, you're making art. Each tweak or gadget is like giving yourself permission to experiment, to get weird (in a good way), and to put your own spin on an old-school craft. It's wild how something as simple as a coil of pine needles can turn into something downright gorgeous with a few personal touches.

Building Your Basketry Kit

So you've wrestled with pine needles and lived to tell the tale. What's next? Time to put together your own basketry kit. And I'm not talking about some boring plastic tub—make it a vibe. Could be a wooden box that looks like it's hiding wizard secrets, a battered canvas bag, or even that old cookie tin you keep meaning to throw out. The point is, you want a spot that's just for your basket stuff—a little creative HQ you can grab whenever inspiration hits. Whether you're chilling at home, heading to a group class, or sneaking in some "me time" on a trip, having your kit ready means you can just get right into it, no fuss.

What goes in the kit? Whatever works for you, honestly, but here's a starter pack: your go-to needles (some people swear by a fat tapestry needle, others like a curved one that fits just right in your hand), a sharp pair of scissors (don't use your kitchen ones, trust me), and an awl for poking holes and wrangling stubborn coils. Threads? Go wild. Waxed linen if you want it tough, embroidery floss when you're feeling flashy, raffia for that "straight-from-the-forest" look. As for the pine needles themselves, treat 'em right—if you're going to use them soon, keep them wrapped in a damp cloth. For later, stash your cleaned and dried needles in a mesh bag so they don't get moldy or weird. And let's be real, as you get better at this, your kit's going to grow. Maybe you'll add some funky beads, dip into dyes, or find cool bits for basket centers (gourds, stones, whatever catches your eye). Your kit becomes this evolving, personal stash that tells your crafting story as much as the baskets themselves.

You know what's wild? Pine needle basketry, along with a bunch of old-school crafts, just oozes this down-to-earth charm. It's the sort of hobby that laughs in the face of fancy gear and overpriced starter kits. No need for a home studio or some weird resin that smells like a chemical spill—just you, a handful of basic tools (most of which you can probably dig out of a junk drawer), and whatever nature decided to drop at your feet that day. If you're putting together your kit, you're not just prepping for a single afternoon of weaving. You're basically buying yourself a ticket to an ongoing, mellow creative adventure. This is the kind of thing that can stick with you for ages, getting richer and more satisfying every time you sit down to coil up another basket.

But here's the real kicker: those simple tools and scruffy little pine needles? They're the bridge between "just stuff lying around outside" and actual art. Think about it—a pine needle, which yesterday was getting trampled by squirrels, is suddenly the backbone of a craft that's been passed down for generations. Once you get your hands on those raw ingredients, you're not just making containers to chuck your keys in. Each basket is its own little story. It's a tribute to the patience you're growing, the skills you're sharpening, and let's be honest, the stubbornness it takes to keep going when your thread tangles for the tenth time.

Chapter 4: Starting the Coil—The Basket Foundation

Look, nobody builds a skyscraper on a mud puddle. Even a halfway decent house needs a solid slab, right? Same deal goes for basketry. That first coil? It's everything. It's the difference between "wow, that looks legit" and "uh, is that supposed to be a hat?" The way you wrap those first pine needles and whip in the stitches sets the whole vibe for your basket—how sturdy it feels, whether it's gonna stand proud or flop over like a sad pancake.

Right from the jump, you're making big calls: How thick do you want your coils? Go chunky, and your basket's got some serious heft. Go skinny, and you're looking at something way more delicate. Even that first circle—how tight you make it, how fast you let it grow—decides if your basket's gonna spread out wide and shallow, or go tall and deep like a little pine needle fortress. Not gonna lie, if you're new to this, that first coil can feel like you're defusing a bomb. But hang in there, because with some stubbornness (and a little swearing), it becomes second nature.

Honestly, if you take away one thing, let it be this: slow your roll. Seriously. This isn't a speed-run. Rushing will make your stitches slip, your coils go wobbly, and, worst case, the whole thing unravels like a bad hair day. Take your time with the foundation. Breathe. Make it count. You're not just slapping together a basket—you're setting yourself up for a project that'll actually make you proud to show it off, warts and all. And yeah, the real magic happens when you build it up, one careful coil at a time, straight from the heart.

Alright, let's ditch the stiff museum-guide vibe and actually talk pine needle basketry like a real person who's spent too many hours poking their fingers with tapestry needles.

First off, you've basically got two main ways to kick off a pine needle basket, and each one's got its own flavor. The purist route? That's making your center out of just pine needles. No bells, no whistles, just a tiny, super-tight coil of needles wound into itself. It's kind of beautiful— raw, earthy, and a little stubborn if you're new to this. You're wrestling with the needles to get 'em flat, toughing it out for that all-natural, no-cheat look. Honestly, it's not the easiest start for beginners, but if you nail it, people will think you're a wizard or something.

Then there's the "let's make life easier (and maybe fancier)" method: slap a decorative or functional base in the middle. Could be a slice of wood drilled with holes, a cool ceramic disk, half a walnut shell if you're feeling rustic, even some random thing you picked up on a hike. These bases? Total game-changer. They give you a solid, steady spot to start coiling, which—let's be real—makes things way less stressful for newbies. Plus, they look cool and give your basket some mixed-media cred. You get to show off your pine needle skills and your taste in found objects all at once. Either way, what matters is you're making a solid, stable core, 'cause if you don't, your basket's gonna end up sad and floppy.

Making a Natural Pine Needle Center

Let's talk about that all-natural pine needle center—because, hey, it's a classic for a reason. You wanna start with pine needles that are actually bendy, not crunchy. Soak 'em in warm water for a while (like, an hour or two) until they're nice and flexible. No one likes a basket full of snapped needles.

Grab a small batch, maybe six to eight needles, and chop off those crusty capped ends—the bit that used to be stuck to the tree. Trust me, don't skip this. If you leave 'em on, your coil gets all lumpy and weird, which is not the vibe.

Line those needles up so the cut ends are all flush. That's your core. Now, grab your thread—raffia if you want the organic look, waxed linen if you're going for smooth and sturdy, or sinew if you're feeling old-school and want bragging rights about durability. Thread up your big, blunt needle and leave yourself a long tail. You'll thank yourself when you're tying off later and things aren't unraveling in your lap.

Now, just start wrapping. Get that thread snug around your little pine needle bundle a bunch of times—tight enough so nothing's sliding around, but don't Hulk-smash it. This first bit is the make-or-break zone. Once you've got it secure, you're off and running, turning a handful of needles into something actually impressive.

And that's it. The magic's in the start. Get your anchor right, and the rest of the basket's a breeze (well, sort of).

So once you've got that bundle all wrapped up and wrangled into submission, it's time for the fiddly bit—bending the thing into a tight little spiral. Think snail shell vibes, or like the swirl you see in the middle of a hurricane from those satellite pics. That first twist? Yeah, that's gonna be the dead center of your basket's base. You just keep nudging those stubborn needles into a circle, stitching as you go. Jam your needle right through the middle of your baby spiral, then whip it around the outside of the coil and yank the thread tight. It'll fight back a little—those needles have a mind of their own and want to snap straight. Don't rush this; just work slow, tweak your grip, and cinch each stitch down. If you let it get wobbly now, your whole base will look off later. Trust me, you'll thank yourself for being fussy here.

Now, after you've conquered your first lap around the spiral, you've got to keep that bundle thick. That means shoving in fresh needles as the old ones get skinny and start to disappear. Always tuck the cut ends deep inside the bundle—nobody wants scratchy bits sticking out. That way, the soft, pointy ends show on the outside, which looks clean and tidy. If you slack off here, your coil will get thin and sad, and the basket might go all flimsy on you.

As your spiral grows, just keep stitching around and around. Every stitch locks the new row of needles to the one underneath and makes that base a little wider. The trick? Keep your stitches even and not too tight. If you yank too hard, the basket will start to pucker or get all stiff and weird. But if you space them out too much, the base will feel loose. Don't sweat it—after a while, you get a rhythm going, and suddenly you're cruising along, making this flat, sturdy base that's just begging for basket walls.

Using Decorative or Functional Centers

Now, about those fancy or, honestly, just way easier centers—some folks (especially if you're new to this whole pine needle scene) like to skip the drama of starting with a fussy little coil. Instead, you grab a ready-made center and just build off that. Way less headache, and you get a cool focal point, too.

People use all sorts of things: slices of walnut shell (which look super classy, by the way), round wooden disks (bonus points if you burn a design into 'em), bits of pottery, even big, funky buttons. If it's flat, rigid, and not too big, you can probably use it. I've seen agate slices, chunks of sea glass, and little metal coins all work their magic here. These give you a rock-solid base to start from—no more wrestling with a wobbly coil. Plus, they make your basket look like you planned the whole thing out, even if you're totally winging it.

Here's how it really goes down with those prepped centers—honestly, it's way easier than you'd think. First, just grab a needle that can handle your thread of choice (waxed linen, sinew, whatever you're feeling). Either poke that sucker through one of the holes in your center piece, or if you're staring at a solid disc, just get ready to wrap your thread right around the edge. No stress.

Thread it up, tie a tough little knot—double up if you're feeling paranoid about it slipping out. Give it a tug. If it holds, you're golden. Now you can actually start wrangling those pine needles. Lay your first bundle right up against the center, make 'em nice and flat so they don't look funky later. If your center has holes, stitch through the next one; if not, just loop that thread right over the edge and around your needle bundle. The first couple stitches? Yeah, those are kinda make-or-break. If you mess them up, everything's gonna slip or unravel and you'll want to throw it all across the room. So, don't mess them up. Once that's locked in, you're basically just coiling and stitching like normal, working out from that solid anchor instead of wrestling with some sad, collapsing spiral.

And here's the real magic: this method saves you from that tiny, fiddly, pain-in-the-butt spiral start. Anyone who's ever tried to wrestle a bunch of pine needles into a neat little coil knows what I'm talking about—it slips, it unravels, it's a disaster. The prepped center? Skips all that drama. Plus, you get to flex your creative muscles way sooner. Imagine the center's a slick polished stone, or some painted medallion with your favorite doodle, or a wood disc with a carved fox or whatever you're into. Suddenly your basket isn't just a basket— it's got attitude, a story, maybe even a little ego.

For newbies, this is a lifesaver. That solid center holds everything together, so you can actually focus on getting your coil thickness and stitch tension right instead of cursing at the foundation AND the stitching. Trust me, it's a way better learning curve.

Once you get the hang of it, you might even start mixing things up—like, start with a wooden base for some structure, then switch halfway through to free-form coiling and let the pine needles do their wild thing. You get the best of both worlds: that solid, steady start, and the artsy, natural vibe later on.

At the end of the day, it's totally up to you—go with a ready-made center or jump into the deep end with a traditional spiral.

Pick whatever suits your mood, your materials, or just the random story you want your basket to tell. That's the real fun of it: it's all yours, every time.

Securing and Expanding the Foundation

Alright, you've got your first round of pine needle basket coiling done—hey, that's something to celebrate. It might look like just a tiny ring, but trust me, getting those first stitches snug and even is already a mini victory. Now, here comes the real gauntlet: actually expanding that little circle into an actual basket. This is when things start to get real, and honestly? It's where a lot of folks start cursing under their breath. Suddenly, your stitches might go all loosey-goosey, or your basket starts looking more like a lopsided UFO than anything you'd want to show off. Been there, done that. But if you keep your eyes peeled and don't rush, it's totally fixable—just part of the learning curve, nothing to cry about.

Here's the not-so-hidden secret: you've gotta find your groove. Every stitch needs to mean something. Imagine you're dancing, but with your fingers and a bunch of pine needles—each move connects the new coil to the last. The spacing? That's where people trip up. Go too wide, and you'll get these awkward gaps that make the basket floppy. Too tight, and the whole thing puckers and goes wonky. You want it just right—pull snug, but not so tight you're strangling the poor thing. Like tying your shoes: secure, but don't cut off circulation. That's the sweet spot. Once you nail that, your basket will start looking a lot less like a Pinterest fail.

As you spiral outward, don't space out and forget to add more pine needles into your bundle. Seriously, this is the rookie mistake to end all rookie mistakes. You get into the zone, stitching away, and suddenly your coil is thinning out like a bad haircut. It looks weird, it feels flimsy, and honestly, it's a pain to fix. So, always have extra needles prepped and ready to go. The minute you notice your bundle losing a bit of thickness, slide in a new needle or two—ideally ones that match what you've already got going on. Just poke 'em right into the core and keep moving. It's way easier than having to backtrack and patch things up later.

Another thing—and people always forget this—keep that base flat. If you pull your stitches up, your basket's gonna start curling into a bowl way before you want it to. You're just trying to make the bottom right now, not a weird half-pipe. So, loosen up your grip a little. Let those coils spread out. And every so often, just press the basket flat against your table (or, let's be real, your lap if you're watching Netflix at the same time). That way you'll feel if it's starting to warp and you can catch it before it turns into a disaster. After a bit of practice, you'll just know by feel how much tension and angle you need—like muscle memory, but for basket nerds.

Eventually, after a few inches, you'll notice the base feels solid—like hey, this thing isn't falling apart in my hands. That's when you can finally relax a bit. Getting the foundation right is easily the trickiest part; after that, the rest of the basket becomes way more chill. By then, you'll have a rhythm going: stitch, add a coil, feed in some needles, repeat. The first few rounds might feel suuuper slow and fiddly, but once you get past that? It speeds up, you'll feel more confident, and suddenly you're not sweating every single stitch. Now you're just cruising, and the basket pretty much builds itself. And if it's still looking a little wonky? Eh, that's just "artisanal charm."

So, here's the deal—your foundation? It ain't just the "bottom" or the spot you kick things off. It's basically your sensei. Those first fat loops? That's where you actually figure out what your particular pine needles wanna do when you yank on them. Some will snap, some will flex, some just… vibe. And don't even get me started on how every thread's got its own personality—tighten one too much and it'll bite, leave one loose and your whole thing goes floppy. Bottom line: every single move you make in those first rounds is straight-up teaching your fingers what's what. Honestly, just mess around with a bunch of tiny coils at first. You'll get it. Your hands'll start to "remember" the motions, and suddenly, the hard stuff later feels kinda obvious. That muscle memory? It's gold. Doesn't matter if you're making a dinky coaster or some monster basket for laundry—nailing the foundation means you're set for life.

Chapter 5: Stitching Techniques Made Simple (Seriously, Don't Stress)

Let's be real: in pine needle basketry, stitches aren't just, like, fancy knots holding your mess together. Nah, they're the backbone. Without stitches, you're just holding a bunch of crunchy, pokey sticks and wondering what went wrong. It's the act of stitching—over, under, again, again—that turns a pile of pine needles into something you can actually use (and maybe show off to your friends if you're feeling cocky). Whether you're making a tiny coaster for your coffee mug or a basket big enough to hide snacks from your roommate, those stitches are what build up the structure, layer by layer. It's a grind sometimes, yeah, but totally worth it when you see the thing taking shape.

And yeah, when you're starting out, it almost feels like punishment—thread goes in, thread comes out, over and over. It's like meditation if meditation included sore fingers and the occasional swear word. But don't skip it, because every single pass with the needle is basically training your hands. You'll start to notice, "Hey, if I pull a little tighter here, or tilt the needle like this, the basket looks way better." It's wild how tiny tweaks change everything— the feel, the look, all of it. Before you know it, you're not just stitching. You're making art. (Or at least, you'll feel like you are.)

But wait, there's more. Stitches aren't just for holding stuff together. They're your chance to flex a little. Pick a wild thread color, change up the stitch, space 'em out, stack 'em—suddenly, your basket's got a vibe. Want to go classic? Use raw raffia and keep it earthy. Feeling extra? Go neon with a crazy figure-eight or blanket stitch and watch people's jaws drop. Seriously, you don't need to master a million techniques—just a few basics, then mess around with colors and patterns. You'll end up with baskets nobody else could ever make, unless they're straight-up copying your style, which, hey, flattery, right?

The Basic Coil Stitch

Alright, so let's just get real about the basic coil stitch. This isn't just some random step in pine needle basketry—it's the thing. The granddaddy. Without this, you're not making a basket, you're just poking at pine needles and getting annoyed. Honestly, if you can't nail this stitch, you're not going anywhere. But hey, no pressure, right?

So here's how it kicks off: You grab your thread (raffia, sinew, linen, whatever you vibe with), thread up your needle, and get ready to roll. You gotta anchor that thread tight to your starting bundle of pine needles—which, by the way, is just a tiny, stubborn little knot of needles that will try to escape if you let it. Get it snug. No one wants a wobbly basket that falls apart the second you look at it sideways.

Now, here comes the part where your hands do the talking. Grab another little bundle of pine needles (a little damp helps them behave, trust me), line it up with your first coil, keep it neat. You're aiming for zero gaps—think of it like laying subway tiles, but, you know, with pine needles and a whole lot more poking yourself with a needle. Shove your blunt tapestry needle through the previous coil, just under where the last thread's wrapped or right through the needle core if you're feeling bold. Yank the thread tight—not so tight you give the needles a complex, just enough to lock that new bundle right up against the old one. Then, you do it again. And again. Stitch, pull, repeat, let it spiral out and up until—ta-da—basket.

Now, here's the secret—consistency is king. Messy stitches? Your basket will look like it got in a fight with a squirrel. Too loose? Gaps everywhere, and your basket's flopping over like a sad pancake. Too tight? You'll end up with a curly, weird bowl that won't sit flat. You want that Goldilocks tension—snug, but not strangled. It's one of those things that just clicks after a while. You get in the groove, your hands start doing the work, and suddenly, you're staring at a basket that looks... kinda awesome.

What's cool about this stitch is you don't have to be a master right away. It's beginner-friendly, because you only have to focus on the basics: keep your stitches even, watch your tension, and shape those coils. Forget fancy colors or beads for now. Once you're comfortable, you can start showing off—fancy threads, beads, crazy angles, all that jazz. But even if you stick with the plain old coil, you can make baskets that are gorgeous and actually useful. People have been doing this forever, and honestly, sometimes the simplest stuff is the prettiest. Master this, and you're golden. The rest is just extra.

Decorative Stitches

Okay, let's be real for a second—sure, the basic coil stitch is like the bread and butter of basketry. It's the thing that holds your basket together (literally), but honestly, it's not what gets people excited. The real fun kicks in with the fancy, decorative stitches. That's where you get to let your freak flag fly. These stitches aren't just about making things pretty—they're what give a basket its vibe, its personality. Without them, you're basically stuck with a glorified plant pot. But start weaving in some decorative flair and suddenly, boom, you've got a statement piece. Plus, it's not just eye candy: a well-placed decorative stitch can beef up the whole structure, making your basket tougher while looking like something you'd see in a museum.

Let's talk about the wheat stitch first, because, honestly, it deserves its hype. Unlike the basic oversew, which is sort of a "get in, get out" deal, the wheat stitch has a little drama to it. You don't just jab your needle straight through. Nah, you angle that sucker, looping the thread over the previous one before tucking it in. It ends up looking like neat rows of tiny wheat—kind of poetic, honestly. And it's not just for show. All those angled, overlapping stitches make the basket feel chunkier and tougher, like it could survive getting tossed around a bit. Plus, it just looks rad. Three-dimensional, textured, the whole works.

Now, the V-stitch—super popular, and for good reason. It's not rocket science, but it makes your basket look like you actually know what you're doing. The trick is in the angle—push the needle through the top, bring it out at an angle, and you get these little "V" shapes marching along your coils. It's neat, organized, and honestly, it's kind of satisfying to see them line up so perfectly. Wanna show off a little? Mess around with thread colors. Swap them every few stitches, or every coil, and suddenly your plain V-stitch is popping with stripes, checkerboards, or whatever wild combo you dream up. Zero extra effort, all the extra style.

But hey, don't box yourself in—there's a whole world of wild stitches out there if you're feeling adventurous. The lazy squaw stitch, for example, gives you this laid-back, almost diagonal pattern that really spreads out. Or try the diamond stitch if you're in the mood for something fancier and geometric—those little diamonds can make your basket look seriously pro. And honestly, there's no end to the variations out there. Some are traditional, some are just made up by people who got bored one afternoon.

Look, the best move? Don't stress about learning every single stitch from the jump. Nail the basic coil stitch first. Get your tension right, make your stitches even, and once you've got that down, then start playing around with the fancy stuff. Each time you try a new stitch, it's not just muscle memory—you're actually building up your skills, figuring out what looks cool, and finding your own style. Before you know it, you're not just making baskets. You're making art. One weird, wonderful stitch at a time.

Getting the Hang of Rhythm and Control

Alright, here's the real deal: the basic coil stitch is like the bones of any coiled basket. It's what keeps the thing upright and not flopping over like a sad pancake. But, honestly, the magic happens once you bring in those fancy decorative stitches. That's where the whole thing jumps from "grandma's utility basket" to "oh wow, you made THAT?" territory. These stitches do double duty—not just holding your basket together (so it doesn't unravel the second you look at it funny), but also jazzing up the surface with cool patterns. The way you mess with the path, tension, or how you twist your thread— whether you're looping, wrapping, or crossing it—can totally flip the vibe of your basket. Suddenly, it's not just a container; it's basically your story woven in fiber.

Let's talk about wheat stitch. People are obsessed with this one and for good reason—it's got this earthy, classic look that just screams "I know what I'm doing." Instead of just yanking the thread straight through the coil, you tilt your needle and cross it over the last working thread before popping it into the next coil. Sounds fiddly, but it's worth it. You end up with this wavy, braided look, like miniature wheat fields swaying in the breeze. Corny metaphor, but it fits. Plus, it's tough as nails—extra overlap means your basket will survive whatever you throw at it (within reason; maybe don't use it for bowling balls).

Then there's the V-stitch, which is basically the go-to for a clean, snappy look. You angle your thread to make these little upside-down V's, marching along the basket like a line of tiny birds. Super satisfying. It's repetitive, which is great if you're a fan of zoning out while you work, but it never looks boring. And if you wanna get wild, switch up the thread colors— alternate them every V, or every few stitches, and suddenly it's a party. Even if you're new to decorative stitches, this one's a solid pick. Low effort, high reward.

Honestly, there's a whole universe of stitches out there. You've got the lazy squaw stitch (yeah, the name's a bit outdated, but the stitch is solid), diamonds, Navajo, links… it's endless. Just a heads-up—don't try to learn them all at once or you'll fry your brain. The smart move? Nail down that basic coil stitch first. Get your hands used to the feel, learn how tight is too tight (or not tight enough), and let that muscle memory kick in. Once the basics feel easy, then you can start tossing in a decorative stitch or two. Every time you practice, you're not just going through the motions—you're picking up skills and, honestly, finding your own style. Before you know it, your baskets start looking less like practice runs and more like something you'd actually want to show off.

Chapter 6: Shaping Your Basket

Okay, let's get real for a second—a pine needle basket isn't just some random container you toss your keys in. Nah, it's like a little autobiography written in needles and thread. The shape? That's the headline. You see a squat, flat basket and think, "Oh, hey, that's for hot bread or maybe grandma's famous pie." But then you spot a basket that's all tall and narrow at the neck, and suddenly it's got secrets, it's hiding stuff—maybe apples, maybe treasure, who knows.

And, honestly, shaping the thing is where the real wizardry happens. You're taking a bunch of pine needles that, on their own, would just sit there looking sad, and you're giving them a whole new life. It's like turning flour and water into bread. Magic, right?

Now, if you're new to this, you're probably obsessed with getting your stitches perfect. Backstitch, whipstitch, that fancy lace stitch—sure, they matter. But if you ignore the overall shape, all you've got is a pretty mess. A basket with good lines? That's the mark of someone who actually knows what they're doing. It's not just about looking pretty, either. If your basket's got solid walls and a steady base, it'll actually work—hold fruit, look good in the middle of the table, whatever you want.

Getting the shape right isn't about some big, dramatic move. It's all these tiny choices adding up. The angle where you stack your next coil (want it tall? Steepen the angle; want it to spread out? Keep it shallow). How tight you pull each stitch— yank it in, the basket narrows; ease off and it grows out. A chunky bundle of needles? The wall gets beefy fast. And, heads up, every little change totally shifts the basket's attitude. At first, you'll probably make these changes without even meaning to and end up with a wonky, lopsided bowl. Welcome to the club. But after some practice, you start to call the shots instead of just reacting to the weird bumps.

So, where do you start? Four basic shapes: flat disc, shallow dish, deep pot, and the classic lidded vessel. Nail those and you've got the muscle memory for anything wild you want to try later. Vases, curvy bowls, stuff that looks like it belongs in a museum—you can mess around all you want once you get the basics down. But every time, it's the same game: you, those pine needles, and a bunch of tiny decisions, all adding up to something that actually says something.

Basically, shaping a basket is part craft, part control freak, and part storyteller. And honestly? That's what makes it cool.

Building Flat and Shallow Forms

Alright, let's get real about coil basketry. Flat shapes? Total no-brainer and honestly, they're where everyone should start. Why? 'Cause you're not wrestling with weird curves or wobbly sides—just pure, simple geometry. Less stress, more room to focus on actually getting your stitches even and not stabbing yourself with a needle (been there, done that). Plus, it's kinda zen, just going round and round, feeling the texture, tweaking the tension until it feels right under your fingers.

These flat forms? Super useful. Think: coasters that don't look like sad cardboard circles, or trivets for those "I swear this pan isn't that hot" moments. Or go artsy and slap one on your wall—bam, instant upgrade. You get to show off your material and stitch game without having to wrangle a 3D shape that looks like a lopsided hat.

Now, if you want your flat basket to actually stay flat (not morph into some weird potato chip), you gotta pay attention. Each coil lines up right next to the last—no sneaky angles, no upward drift. Picture stacking donuts, not building a Leaning Tower of Pisa. Stitches should be tight enough to hold it together, but if you're pulling like you're in some sort of thumb war, the whole thing will start to curl up or pucker. If you catch the edge doing a little wave or cupping, chill out on the tension for a bit, or use your thumb to gently press the coil down as you go. Seriously, flatness is great—don't let it get away from you.

Once you nail the flat stuff, shallow bowls are the next adventure. Same idea, but you start sneaking the coil up, just a hair. I'm talking, like, a millimeter per round. No sudden moves—unless you're aiming for an accidental modern art piece. You want the sides to glide up, not jut out like a bad haircut.

And hey, consistency is the name of the game. Don't let one side climb higher than the other or you'll end up with a basket that looks like it's had a rough night out. Every so often, stop and put your basket on a flat surface. Spin it around, eyeball the sides—make sure it's not trying to take off. If you see a wonky spot, adjust: loosen the stitches where it's getting too eager, pull tighter where it's lagging behind, or even mess with the coil thickness. Thicker coil equals more lift. Thinner flattens things out. Don't be afraid to smoosh and nudge the coil a bit before you stitch. Your hands are the boss here.

So yeah, coil basketry: start flat, get shallow, and don't be afraid to get your hands dirty. That's where the good stuff happens.

There's just something about shallow baskets. They look all delicate and simple, but honestly, that's just the start. These little guys are basically the Swiss Army knives of the basket world. Toss your keys in by the front door? Yup. Stash jewelry on your dresser? Absolutely. Dump a load of wrapped candy in there and boom— instant "I'm-a-cool-host" vibes for your guests. They even wrangle all that random desk nonsense—paper clips, hair ties, rogue chapsticks. And don't even get me started on using them as a practice playground for rookie basket makers. Perfect for figuring out how to go from a pancake-flat base to a nice, gentle curve (which, by the way, is the big secret behind all the fancier baskets you'll want to make later). Nail the shallow bowl, and suddenly you're not just making baskets— you're building confidence to tackle the big, wild stuff.

Creating Deep and Rounded Baskets

Now, let's talk about deep and rounded baskets. This is where things get a little spicy. The big difference? You gotta pay way more attention to the angle of your coils. Like, if you want your basket to actually get taller instead of just wider, you've gotta start aiming those coils upward as soon as you leave the base behind. No more lazy, almost-flat stacking. Push those coils up. Every round, just a little more vertical. Suddenly, what started as a placemat is growing into a three-dimensional masterpiece.

Here's the catch: as your basket climbs higher, every tiny inconsistency starts to shout a little louder. If your stitches are all over the place, or your coils are thick here and skinny there, or you get sloppy with your angles, you're gonna notice. The walls might bulge out like they just ate a big lunch, or suck in like they're holding their breath. Sometimes that's actually cool—some of the best traditional baskets have those wobbly, organic curves. But if you're aiming for that crisp, straight-sided look? Yeah, you'll have to get fussy. Constantly check your basket against something vertical—a box, a wall, whatever's handy—so you can spot any weirdness before it gets out of hand. Then just tweak your coil or your stitches next time around. Basket-making: part art, part obsessive measuring contest.

And if you're feeling extra ambitious, try a rounded basket. These things are like the ballerinas of the basket world—graceful, curvy, a little dramatic. You start by flaring those coils outward, giving the basket its "belly." Once you hit peak chonk, you gotta start curving things back in, drawing the coils inward toward the rim. The whole trick is to make that transition smooth, so you don't end up with a basket that looks like it's got a weird dent or a sudden hip. When you get it right, it's like you've channeled the spirit of a gourd, a clay pot, or even a human silhouette. It's not easy, but hey, once you've got it down, you can make baskets that'll make people stop and stare. And isn't that the dream?

You know what gets totally ignored way too often? Bundle thickness. Seriously, nobody talks about it enough, but it can make or break a deep basket—both how tough it is and how it looks sitting on your table. Think about it: whatever you're coiling up (raffia, pine needles, random grasses, old shoelaces if you're feeling wild), you've gotta bundle that stuff up to make your coil's "spine." Go thick, and you're basically building the Hulk of baskets. Thick bundles mean the walls are solid, chunky, and give off those "I could survive the apocalypse in here" vibes. But—no surprise—it's like wrangling a garden hose if you're trying to make tight corners or fancy shapes. Kinda limits your options for getting all intricate.

Now, thin bundles? Whole different story. You can twist and bend them into all sorts of delicate curves, super tight circles, and even get into that ultra-fine detail work. Downside is, they're wimpy on their own. You'll need to stitch the coils more often and way tighter, or maybe sneak in a second, hidden coil just to keep the thing from flopping apart.

Here's where it gets fun—seasoned basket folks don't just pick one or the other. Nah, they mix it up. Like, thick coils down at the bottom, so the base is sturdy and doesn't sag. Then, as they move up and want to get a nice, swoopy belly or a rim that tapers off all dainty, they'll switch to slim bundles. Sometimes they'll even beef it up again at the top for a rim that doesn't give up after one rough grocery run. Playing with thickness lets you build a basket that's both strong and pretty dang pretty—kind of like the Swiss Army knife of baskets.

Finishing Touches and Functional Additions

Now, about those final touches—this is where the magic happens, honestly. You can have a basket that's all structure and no style, but if you want something that actually looks finished and not like you just gave up halfway through, you've gotta nail the rim and other details. The rim isn't just the end of the basket—it's the exclamation point. Get it right, and suddenly your basket looks intentional, like you actually meant for it to turn out that way.

To get that slick, pro-level rim, you gotta taper off your bundle at the end. Basically, keep thinning it out stitch by stitch, peeling off a few needles every time, so the final coil just melts into the rest. No weird chunky ends sticking out. Then, lock that sucker down with a bunch of tiny, super-tight stitches. And hey, before you call it done, check for any rogue needles poking out. Tuck them in or snip them off— nobody wants a basket that bites.

If you're feeling extra, toss in some handles or a lid. Handles are clutch if you actually want to carry the thing, or just want to flex with a little basket bling. Usually, you leave a gap in your coil, then bridge it with more pine needles, stitching like crazy so it's strong enough to survive the trip from car to kitchen (or wherever you're showing this beauty off). Handles can be low-key little grips, or go big with fancy arches—totally up to you. If you're hauling heavy stuff, maybe reinforce the handle core with something tougher, or just double up the stitches so you don't end up with a busted handle.

Bottom line: bundle thickness isn't just a technical detail, it's your secret weapon for making baskets that are both tough and gorgeous. And those finishing touches? That's the difference between "I made this in a rush" and "Check out this masterpiece."

Let's talk about lids. This is where things get tricky—no winging it here, unless you're cool with a wobbly, lopsided cover that pops off if you look at it funny. You've gotta nail the measurements, match the curve of the basket rim, and basically play Tetris with your materials. Sometimes that means making a lid that's flat as a pancake, or maybe you go all out and sculpt this dramatic, domed thing that looks like it belongs in a fancy bento box. Building a domed lid? Start with a flat circle, then slowly ramp up your coils as you spiral out—basically building a basket, but upside down. Weirdly satisfying, honestly. And if you're feeling extra, toss in a ridge or lip on the underside so the lid locks in place instead of just sitting there, taunting you. Some folks even stitch on a hinge, which is basically basketry wizardry.

Now, decoration—that's where you get to flex. It's not just about slapping on some flashy bits to distract from mistakes (okay, sometimes it is), but more about using color and texture to highlight the good stuff. Maybe you stitch a bold, dark band around the rim, and boom—your basket suddenly looks taller and fancier than it really is. Or you bead up the widest point of a round belly basket, so it looks extra plump and juicy, like a peach you wanna grab off the table. Little details like that— contrasting threads, pops of color, shiny beads—they do more than just pretty things up. They show off your skills, your eye for detail, and honestly, your patience. Because, let's be real, this stuff takes forever.

Speaking of patience—yeah, that's the real secret sauce. Rush through a basket and it's gonna show: lopsided, tension all over the place, weird gaps where you lost focus. The best baskets? They look effortless, but only because someone spent hours (days?) fussing over every stitch, nudging each coil into place, fixing every tiny mistake until it's juuust right. That's what separates the "meh" from the masterpieces. You take your time, respect the process, and in the end, you've got something that looks gorgeous, feels solid, and gives off that quiet "I know what I'm doing" vibe—even if you were cursing under your breath the whole time.

Chapter 7: Adding Color and Decoration

Why Decoration Matters

Let's be real, pine needle baskets already have this chill, natural beauty going on. There's something about those warm, earthy colors—deep greens, browns, even a bit of gold if you're lucky—that just pulls you in. And the way those coils stack up? It's almost hypnotic. Kinda makes you wanna run your fingers along 'em, right? The handmade vibe is strong. But here's the thing: as awesome as that natural look is, adding your own splash of color or some funky decorations can take a basket from "hey, nice" to "whoa, you made THAT?" Suddenly it's not just a container—it's your container. A little piece of your personality, sitting right there on the table. That's the magic of jazzing things up: it's where you get to play, mess around, and figure out what you like, no rules, just vibes. Especially if you're new to this whole basket weaving thing, decoration is the perfect excuse to experiment. Maybe you'll find a style that's totally you, or maybe you'll just have fun making a mess. Either way, it's all part of the ride.

Decoration isn't just some modern Pinterest trend either—it's old school. Like, really old. All over the world, people have been tricking out their baskets for ages, each culture putting its own spin on things. Some folks keep it super chill, letting the pine needles do the talking. Maybe a little colored thread here, a tiny wrap there—nothing too wild, just enough to catch your eye. Other people? Oh, they go all in. Bright threads, crazy beads, dyed fibers, the whole nine yards. Sometimes those choices mean something—a memory, a family story, the changing seasons, whatever. So yeah, when you add color or decoration, you're telling a story. Maybe it's loud, maybe it's quiet, but it's yours.

Before you break out the rainbow beads and start gluing on glitter (please don't), here's the big secret: the best decoration doesn't drown out what's already beautiful. Those pine needles are already doing a lot of heavy lifting, so you want your extras to play nice. Pick colors and patterns that vibe with the natural shades, not fight 'em. It's about balance. Like, you want your basket to feel put together, not like it lost a fight with a craft store clearance bin. Let the natural beauty shine, and just add a little something-something to make it pop.

And honestly? There's a ton of ways to jazz up a pine needle basket. Maybe you stitch with colored thread—waxed linen, embroidery floss, whatever you've got—just a little accent here or there. Or maybe you dye the needles, go subtle or go wild, totally up to you. Wanna get fancy? Wrap in some raffia, toss in a bit of yarn, maybe even some silk. You can weave in beads, shells, polished stones, heck, even a cool leaf you found on a walk. The trick, especially if you're just getting started, is to keep it simple at first. Try one color, a couple beads, see how you like it. Once you're feeling bold, mix it up. The more you play around, the more your style's gonna show up. And that's when things get really interesting.

Coloring Through Threads and Fibers

Honestly, choosing what you stitch with? It's not just a technical thing—it's where the whole vibe of your basket comes alive. It's like picking your outfit for the day: sure, it keeps you covered, but it also tells the world what you're about. The thread, yarn, or raffia you use isn't just holding pine needles together; it's basically the paintbrush for your basket's personality. Pick bold or weird textures, experiment with colors, and suddenly you're not just making a basket. You're making a statement. A bright zigzag here, some moody dark lines there—next thing you know, your humble bundle of pine needles is looking straight-up fancy.

Let's talk color—because, wow, there's a whole playground here. If you're into the chill, subtle look, go for the neutrals: beige, tan, brown, that sort of thing. It's like letting the pine needles be the star of the show, just a whisper of color so nothing overshadows that wild, natural beauty. Really understated, super classic, and honestly, it never looks outdated. People will squint at your basket and go, "Dang, that's classy."

But if you're like me and sometimes want a basket that screams "look at me!"—bring on the color-bombs. Fiery red, sky blue, neon green, whatever. These colors don't blend in, they shout from across the room. Suddenly, your stitches aren't just doing their job—they're strutting their stuff, stealing the spotlight. You can keep it simple and stick with one color all the way, which gives this really sleek, unified look. Or, if you're feeling artsy, go wild with stripes, bands, or patterns. It almost turns your basket into a storybook, each color a plot twist.

Now, about raffia—this stuff is kind of a superstar in the basket world. It's a natural fiber, straight from the raffia palm (if you're into that handmade, earthy feel). It's tough but bendy, which makes it awesome for wrapping and binding. Plus, it comes in all sorts of colors. Even when dyed, raffia keeps that raw, slightly rustic texture—something synthetic threads just can't fake. And here's a cool trick: you can wrap it tight enough to totally hide the pine needles underneath, laying down thick, solid stripes of color. Do this and suddenly your basket's got attitude, maybe a bold colored base, or a rim that pops, or a fat, dramatic stripe right around the middle. Seriously—if you want to play up the drama or spotlight certain spots, raffia's got your back.

Yarn is a playground for anyone who likes to mess around with textures. If you're the type who just loves the feel of things, swapping in some soft wool or chunky cotton yarn for your basket? It's like turning a regular basket into a squishy cloud you want to keep poking. And if you're feeling a little extra (hey, who isn't sometimes?), you can always throw in some glitzy stuff—metallic threads, shiny silk, whatever catches your eye at the craft store. That little shimmer can take your project from "homemade" to "Wait, did you buy that at Anthropologie?"

But here's the deal: not all yarn is your friend. Some of it is basically just fluff waiting to fall apart. You want to grab something that's got some backbone— think tightly spun yarns, mercerized cotton, linen blends. If you go with the delicate, floofy stuff, your basket's gonna look sad after a few weeks of use. Trust me, you don't want your masterpiece unraveling the first time someone actually touches it.

One of the best things about decking out baskets with threads and fibers? It's ridiculously accessible. Seriously, you don't need to be some kind of fiber arts wizard. Just swap in a new color, or grab a different yarn, and suddenly your basket's got a whole new vibe. It's all about playing around. You'll figure out what you like as you go. Mess around enough and, before you know it, you'll be plotting out crazy spirals, color fades, or geometric patterns that'll make your friends say, "Wait, you made that?" That's when you know you're onto something.

Beads, Shells, and All That Jazz

Look, threads and raffia are cool and all, but if you wanna take your basket from "Hey, nice" to "Whoa, what is THAT?"— you gotta add some bling. Beads, shells, random little trinkets you found in your junk drawer... this is where basketry gets personal.

Beads are basically the MVP of basket embellishments. They're easy, they're everywhere, and you can go subtle or full-on maximalist with them. Thread 'em right onto your stitching or weaving, and boom—suddenly your basket's got rhythm. Glass beads? They catch the light like tiny disco balls. Wood beads? Super earthy, chill, almost like your basket's about to start burning incense and playing folk music. Ceramic or stone beads give some serious weight—literally. Plus, they usually have these cool textures and glazes that make the whole thing feel grounded and handmade. And don't even get me started on the endless variety: matte, shiny, huge, teeny-tiny, smooth, faceted. You can go wild.

Shells are another classic, especially if you've got a thing for beachy vibes. People have been stitching shells into baskets forever—there's just something about that ocean connection. Tiny shells can be tucked right into your coils for little pops of texture. Or go big and dramatic with a honkin' scallop shell or a row of cowries right at the rim. It's like bringing a bit of the beach home—minus the sand everywhere.

Bottom line: get weird, get creative, and don't stress about making it perfect. The best baskets? They're the ones that make you wanna keep running your hands over 'em, discovering all the little surprises you tucked in. That's where the magic happens.

You'd be surprised how deep the world of basket bling goes. We're not just talking beads and feathers—literally anything can get woven in. Stones are a classic move: you can go with a smooth pebble from that river you hiked last summer, a shiny cabochon you found at the flea market, or a gnarly little rock that just looks cool. Each one's got a vibe. And buttons. If you've ever raided your grandma's sewing kit, you know how wild those things can get—old-school mother-of-pearl with that pearly shimmer, or funky new resin buttons in colors that practically shout at you. Tiny metal or clay charms, little animals, weird symbols, whatever—you can stitch 'em in and suddenly your basket's telling its own story. Sometimes it's about how it feels in your hand, sometimes it's a secret meaning just for you or whoever's getting the basket. Kinda like wearable art, but for your coffee table.

Now, here's the trap: more isn't always better. I mean, it's super tempting to slap everything on there—bling it up like a Vegas showgirl. But honestly? That's a one-way ticket to mess-ville. If you go overboard, suddenly your basket looks like it lost a fight with a craft store. Best way to play it is like you're accessorizing for a first date: pick a couple of killer pieces, put them where they'll really pop, and leave it at that. Maybe a neat ring of matching beads around the rim, or just one killer stone smack in the middle—bam, that's the focal point. The trick is to make the basket and the extras work together, so they're not fighting for attention like siblings at Christmas.

Some basket folks get super creative and go all-in on natural bits. Think feathers you found on a hike (not the sketchy ones, please), pressed leaves, dried flowers— stuff that basically brings the outdoors in. Stitch a little fern under the rim, or tuck a sprig of lavender in a coil, and suddenly your basket's got that whole "I just walked through a meadow" energy. Sure, those decorations might not last forever— nature's got a short shelf life—but that's kinda the point. You end up with a basket that captures a season, like autumn leaves or spring blossoms. It's a snapshot, not just a storage container.

And don't even get me started on the meaning behind all this stuff. People love to load baskets with secret codes and stories. Blue beads for calm or water, shells if you're repping your beach roots, stones from your hometown for a little piece of home. Heck, even the colors matter—natural dyes can tell you whether the basket's meant for a wedding, a celebration, or just because someone's obsessed with purple. When you throw in these elements, you're not just making a thing to hold apples. You're making a time capsule, a memory jar, a shout-out to your roots or your hopes or whatever's rattling around in your head. That's the best part, honestly—your hands tell the story, and the basket listens.

Painted and Dyed Pine Needles

So, here's the thing: pine needles are cool on their own, right? That whole earthy, sunbaked vibe they get as they dry—love that for them. But sometimes you just wanna jazz things up, throw in a little color, make your basket pop. That's where dyeing and painting come in.

If you're into dyeing, it's honestly not rocket science. Grab your needles, soak 'em in some water with fabric dye (the messier, the better, I say). After they soak up the color, rinse 'em off and let them dry. You can use all dyed needles for a loud, in-your-face look, or mix 'em with the original brown ones for stripes or color-blocked patterns. Picture this: bright red coils weaving in and out of natural browns—kinda looks like a candy cane, but way less sticky.

Painting? Yeah, you can totally do that too, though it's not as common. It's a bit fiddly—think tiny paintbrushes, maybe some acrylics, and a steady hand. You can go wild with color placement, but don't glob it on or your needles will get all stiff and cranky (and then they flake, which is just gross). Keep it light, leave a little of the needle showing, and you'll be golden.

Look, dyeing and painting open up a world of possibilities, but let's not kid ourselves—they're not always a cakewalk. Keeping colors consistent is tricky, and if you leave your masterpiece in the sun, those vibrant hues might just say "bye." Still, if you're just getting started and want to add some personality to your baskets, this is a fun way to experiment and make your stuff stand out.

Chapter 8: Troubleshooting Common Mistakes

Here's the real talk: pine needle basketry looks super zen and all—like, "oh, just me and my needles, finding inner peace." But, it can be kind of a nightmare when you're new. The needles do whatever they want, your hands cramp up, and your once beautiful coil starts looking like a wobbly pasta noodle.

Even the pros mess up. No joke. You'd think after a hundred baskets, they'd have it down, but nope—sometimes the stitches go all wonky, or the coils loosen up and your basket suddenly has the structural integrity of a wet paper bag. Or bam— some random gap shows up where you least expect it, like a secret door to nowhere.

But honestly? That's just how it goes. These aren't failures—they're just part of learning. Every mistake is basically the universe saying, "Hey, pay attention"

Maybe your stitches are uneven because your tension's all over the place. Needle snapping? Probably didn't soak 'em enough. Basket base wonky? Your coiling rhythm's doing the cha-cha. If you actually look at what went wrong, you pick up way more than you would by just following some tutorial.

And let's be real—everyone gets bummed when their first basket comes out lopsided or the stitches look like they were done by a caffeinated squirrel. You see those perfect baskets online and feel like, "Why do mine look like this?" But here's the thing: handmade stuff isn't supposed to be perfect. That's the whole point. Embrace the weirdness. That's what makes it yours.

Honestly, those little quirks in your stitches or wobbly shapes—don't even stress about 'em. That's not a mistake, that's your basket's vibe, its signature. Like, imagine every tiny weird spot as your own personal fingerprint. It's a shoutout to the day you sat down to weave, what you felt, maybe if you had too much coffee, all of it.

Flawlessness? Kinda overrated, honestly. Chasing perfection is just a recipe for frustration city. The real win is getting better with each attempt and learning to spot those "oops" moments before they even happen. After a while, stuff that used to drive you nuts will just become tiny tweaks—fixable, no drama, almost muscle memory. You'll barely even notice.

Troubleshooting? It's really about stopping problems before they even show up. Most of the time, the stuff that messes up your basket doesn't happen while you're stitching—it happens way before. Skip the prep, and you're basically asking for trouble. Like, if your pine needles are dry as a bone, they'll snap and fight you the whole way. Too-thin thread? It'll fray to bits and look messy. Too chunky? Overpowers the whole thing. And if you're rushing— everyone's been there—you'll end up with a lopsided mess or stitches that just don't hold together. Slow down. Seriously, prep your stuff, check as you go, and you'll dodge half the classic rookie mistakes.

Loose or Uneven Stitches

Let's talk about those loose or weird stitches. This one gets everybody at first. Keeping your tension even is the holy grail of basketry. Not just for looks—if your stitches are all over the place, the whole basket's gonna be a wobbly, sad pancake. Loose stitches? Everything shifts around, gaps pop up, and the basket might just give up and collapse. Nobody wants a floppy basket. On the flip side, yank those stitches too tight, and suddenly your nice round basket is turning into a weird oval, or the opening's shrinking like it's afraid of the world. Sometimes it even pulls in so much it caves in on itself. Plus, super tight stitches can trash your materials and make it a pain to keep going.

So yeah, tension is everything. Finding that sweet spot takes practice, but once you get it, you'll wonder why you ever worried. And don't sweat the imperfections—they're proof you made something real, with your own hands.

So you're staring down a loose stitch. Annoying, right? Here's what I do: just kinda mash the loose coils together with your fingers at first—don't get all Hulk on it, just enough to nudge the gap closed. If it still looks floppy, grab your needle and run a few extra stitches over that spot. Make sure the thread's pulling everything snug, but don't yank like you're trying to wrangle a wild animal, or you'll end up with a wonky, warped basket. If a whole chunk feels wimpy, no shame in beefing it up with extra stitches right between the old ones. Basically, you're just stitching a little denser, giving the whole thing more backbone. After a while, your hands get the hang of it—tight enough to hold, but chill enough to keep the basket looking natural and not like a school project gone wrong.

Now, about those weird, lopsided stitches—honestly, everyone's been there. You look down and some stitches are stretched out like spaghetti, others are squished up like they're in a rush. Usually, it's just because you lost your spot or you started zoning out (or Netflix distracted you, let's be real). The trick? Slow down. Like, actually look at where you're putting each stitch, and check your spacing before you pull the thread through. I know a few basket nerds who use a little ruler or some homemade template to keep things even. Personally, I just eyeball it and check every few stitches—if something looks off, fix it right away before it snowballs.

But hey, if you finish a chunk and realize it's a bit funky, don't panic. You can always slap a little colored raffia or a bead over that spot—it'll look artsy, not accidental. Call it "creative flair."

And here's a secret: once the basket gets bigger, all those little mess-ups basically disappear. In the early stages, every tiny goof is right there in your face, but as you add layers, nobody's gonna notice unless they're examining it with a microscope. Chill out about perfection. Those quirks? That's what makes it look handmade and cool, not some soulless factory job.

Embrace the weirdness. Your basket, your rules.

Gaps, Breaks, and Splits in the Coils

Basket weaving, honestly, is one of those crafts that looks super chill from the outside—like, "Oh, you just coil up some pine needles and voilà, a basket." Yeah, not quite. Even if you've been at it for years, you'll run into the same annoying hiccups as everyone else. Gaps showing up between your coils? Welcome to the club.

Let's talk about those gaps for a sec. Nothing ruins the whole "I made this with my hands." pride like seeing daylight peeking through your hard work. Plus, it's not just about looks—those gaps can make your basket wobbly and weak. So what's going on? Sometimes your pine needles are basically ancient and cranky; if they're dry or brittle, they just don't want to play nice, snapping when you try to bend them snug. Or maybe you're pulling your thread like a wild animal one minute and barely tugging the next. That uneven tension? It'll 100% mess with your basket's vibe, making some spots loose and floppy and others tight as a drum. And, let's be real, sometimes you just forget to smash those coils together as you go. It happens.

Now, about fixing it—hydration is your best friend. Seriously, soak those pine needles in warm water for at least half an hour. If they're extra stubborn, give them a spa day overnight. Keep a wet rag or spray bottle nearby while you work, too, so the needles don't dry out halfway through and start acting up again. And don't just stitch and hope for the best. Every time you add a new coil, use your thumb and finger to smoosh it up tight against the last one before you stitch. It's one of those little habits that makes a world of difference— keeps everything compact and gives your basket that professional, "no air gaps here" look.

But hey, sometimes the problem isn't between the coils—it's inside the coil itself. Ever notice a weird dip or bulge and wonder what the heck happened? Odds are, you mixed needles of all different lengths in your bundle, so the short ones bail early, leaving empty spots. The result: your coil looks like it skipped leg day.

Here's what actually helps: Sort your pine needles before you start. Don't obsess over getting them perfectly matched, just eyeball it and group similar lengths together. When you need to add new needles, don't just slap them on the end— slide them in so they overlap, like you're feathering them into the bundle. That way, the transition's smooth and nobody notices the join. If you still end up with a gap inside the bundle, no big deal—just sneak in another needle (or two) right into the thin patch, weave it in there, and keep stitching. A couple of extra stitches, and it'll blend right in. No one will ever know.

So yeah, basket making's got its drama. But honestly, once you know these tricks, you'll save yourself a lot of frustration— and your baskets will look way less like beginner projects and more like something you'd proudly show off at the next craft fair.

Let's talk about broken pine needles— because honestly, it's like they're out to ruin your day sometimes. Pine needles are tough in the wild, but once you start twisting and bending them around tight curves, they can snap with almost zero warning. Dry air? Yeah, that's a recipe for brittle, snap-happy needles. Forget to keep 'em moist? Good luck. And when they do break, you're left with this ugly little stub poking out, messing up the smooth look of your basket and snagging on stuff. Super annoying.

Quick fix? Just grab your sharpest little scissors and snip off the busted end. Tuck that trimmed bit right under the closest stitches. You wanna kind of sneak it in beneath the coils, keep it low-key so nobody notices your mid-project disaster. Problem solved, at least for minor breaks. If you end up with a bigger gap—like, you could drive a toy car through it—then bring in some backup. Grab some raffia or maybe a funky thread, whatever matches, and stitch across the hole. Whip stitch, figure-eight, whatever works. Bonus: you can make it look intentional, like it's a hip little design element. Fake it 'til you make it, right?

With time, you'll start to get a feel for which needles are about to betray you. Brittle? Weird color? Feels off when you bend it? Chuck it back in water or save it for a spot where it won't matter much. Honestly, the more you mess around with this, the more your hands pick up on these little cues. Patience and touch—can't teach that overnight, but it'll save your sanity and make your baskets look way more pro.

Problems with Shape and Structure

Now, about getting your basket to actually look like, you know, a basket—shaping is a whole different beast. Every newbie wants that perfect, round masterpiece...and then bam, you end up with something that looks like it's melting on one side or trying to become a salad bowl. Flat coasters decide to go full 3D, and suddenly you've got a wobbly UFO.

Honestly, this stuff happens because of a few classic rookie moves. Number one: tension problems. Sometimes you're yanking the thread like you're in a tug-of-war, then you go all loosey-goosey in the next section. Or, maybe your stitches are wandering all over the place—too far, too close, squished, stretched. And let's be real, sometimes you're so into the rhythm you forget to check if your basket is even still basket-shaped. Next thing you know, you've drifted way off course.

So what do you actually do when your basket starts listing like a tiny ship in a storm? Don't panic. Usually, you can squish it back into shape with your hands—especially if your pine needles aren't bone-dry. Give it a little press and nudge as you go. You can fix a lot with just some manual muscle. But if things are really wonky, you might need to bulk up the skinny side. Add another coil or two where it's sagging, or make your coils a little beefier there until things even out. Sometimes you gotta get creative and just boss the basket around a bit.

Bottom line: don't expect perfection right out the gate. Baskets have a mind of their own, and half the fun is learning to wrangle them into shape. Keep at it, don't stress the weird curves, and remember—nobody notices your mistakes as much as you do.

Here's the thing—basket walls just love to do their own thing sometimes. One minute, you think you've got everything tight and tidy, then boom, the sides are flaring out like they just remembered it's the '70s and bell bottoms are cool again. That's usually your stitches being way too chill—loose stitches mean the whole thing just kind of… sprawls. Now, if your basket starts sucking in at the sides, all pinched and narrow, that's your grip going all Hulk on the yarn—too tight, my friend. The trick? Watch your tension like a hawk but, you know, don't stress too much. If your basket's fanning out, yank those stitches in a bit. If it's closing up like a clam, loosen up. Sometimes, I just grab a bowl or a cup and shove my basket-in-progress around it—inside if it's flaring, outside if it's squeezing in. Let the bowl boss the shape for a while. Cheating? Maybe. Effective? Heck yes.

Flat projects—like coasters or those fancy placemats everyone pretends they use—are a whole new circus. You think you're making a pancake, but suddenly it's a flying saucer, edges curling up like it's trying to escape. Nine times out of ten, you're pulling too tight or laying coils all wonky. Happens to the best of us. As soon as you see the curl, chill out on the tension for the next round. Give the material some breathing room. And here's a sneaky move: after every round, just slam that thing flat on the table and press it down. Not too hard—don't squash your masterpiece—just enough to remind it who's boss. Honestly, if you keep at it, most of the time you can flatten things out before it goes full taco shell on you.

And hey, let's get real for a second—perfection is overrated. If you wanted a flawless, soulless basket, you'd just buy one from a factory. Those little wobbles and quirks? That's the good stuff. That's what makes your basket actually yours. Loads of traditional baskets from all over the world are a little lopsided, a bit wonky, and people love them for it. So, don't freak out if things aren't textbook. Enjoy the mess, laugh at the weird shapes, and let your basket have its own personality. Trust me, it's way more fun that way.

Finishing Issues and Rough Edges

Alright, let's get real about finishing your basket—because this is where beginners either totally nail it or end up wanting to throw the whole thing out the window. The final steps, the "finishing," are basically the difference between "Wow, you made that?" and "Oh... you made that." It's wild how much those last few minutes matter. And yeah, this is also where a ton of rookie mistakes pop up, so don't beat yourself up if you mess it up the first (or tenth) time.

First up: those last stitches. People are so focused on the body of the basket, by the time they hit the end, they're like, "Eh, I'll just snip this thread, whatever." Nope. That's a rookie move. If you just tie a sad little knot and trim it, guess what? That sucker's gonna work loose, and you'll end up with a floppy, unraveling mess. Not cute. You gotta tie a solid, tight knot right up against the last coil, pull it firm, and then—here's the secret sauce—grab a sharp needle and weave that tail back under at least three or four existing stitches. Bury it in there, deep. Especially if you're using raffia (which is kinda grippy anyway), this locks everything down. Once it's tucked and hidden, then you can trim it off so it's flush. It's a little fussy, but honestly, it's worth it. That clean finish? Chef's kiss. It just makes the whole basket feel legit.

Now, the rim. Ugh, the number of times I've poked myself on a janky rim. It's usually because some needle tip or stiff thread end is sticking out like a tiny splinter, waiting to jab you. The trick is to be super mindful as you do those last rounds. Angle your needle so it tucks under the outer layer, not just stabbing straight through. Hide the sharp stuff inside the coil. But, you know, sometimes you finish and the rim still feels like a cactus. No biggie. If you're using stuff like pine needles or reed, just grab some fine sandpaper (220 grit or higher—don't go at it with anything rough, unless you want to wreck your hard work) and give it a gentle buff. That usually smooths things out. Or, if you wanna get fancy (or just cover up your sins), wrap the rim with a bit of braided raffia or a decorative twist. Glue it, stitch it, whatever. It hides the ugliness and makes the basket look even cooler. And if the rim's still a disaster? Slap a handle on it, toss on a lid, or add another coil. Half the time, those "oops" fixes end up being the best part.

And, real talk, the emotional side hits hard here too. You finish and your basket's all wobbly, or the tension's wonky, or it just looks... off. Kinda soul-crushing, right? But here's the thing: nobody starts out making perfection. Those first few baskets? They're like snapshots of where you were at that moment. They're proof you tried, learned, and kept going. Most basket makers I know keep their first disasters on a shelf like trophies. They don't see failure—they see progress. Honestly, that's the magic of this craft. Every wonky, lopsided, slightly tragic basket is a step forward, and if you keep at it, you'll see the difference. Perfection's overrated anyway.

Give me something with character and a story every time.

Chapter 9: Finishing and Caring for Your Basket

Alright, here's the part where things get real. You've spent ages coiling, stitching, fussing over every little detail, and now— just when you think you're done—the finish line sneaks up and dares you to mess it all up. No pressure, right? But honestly, this last step's where your basket either goes from "Hey, cool pine needles" to "Whoa, did you actually make that?" Or, on the flip side, a sloppy finish can turn your masterpiece into something you'd rather hide in the closet. Doesn't matter if your stitches are on point and the shape is chef's kiss—if the rim is janky or you've got loose ends flapping around, it's gonna look like you quit halfway through. Plus, sloppiness now means your basket might unravel later, and who wants to watch their hard work fall apart? Not me.

So, here's how you nail the finish: When you're about to close up, grab those last few inches of your pine needle bundle and start thinning it out. I'm talking about slowly yanking out a couple of needles at a time, so you get this soft, feathered taper instead of a sudden, chunky lump. Seriously, don't just chop it off or you'll have a weird, stubby rim that screams "rookie." Once you've got your nice skinny end, tuck it underneath a few stitches from the previous coil—kind of like hiding the last bit of wrapping paper under the present. Pull your thread nice and tight, and boom, the end's invisible. You want everything tucked away: no poky needles, no rogue threads. It's like hiding your dirty laundry before guests come over.

After you've done the tucking bit, you have to knot your thread. This is non-negotiable—skip it and you'll regret it when the whole thing starts unraveling while you're showing it off. Make a small, tight knot and jam it up against the inside of the basket or some spot where it won't catch the spotlight. What you use for thread makes a difference, too. If you're using raffia, that stuff's got grip—run the end through a few coils with a needle, and it'll stay put. Waxed linen or sinew? They're sticky, so a double knot and a quick tuck under a stitch or two should do the trick. Just promise me you'll double-check everything. Run your fingers around the rim, squish it a bit—if anything feels wobbly or loose, fix it now, not later.

Want to be extra fancy? Go for a decorative wrap around the rim. Grab some contrast thread or a different fiber—something that pops—and wind it tightly around the edge. Even a simple whipstitch looks crazy professional if you keep it snug and even. Not only does this make your basket look slick, but it also helps beef up the edge so it doesn't wear out. Basically, you're adding armor and bling at the same time. Win-win.

And that's it. Finish strong, and your basket's not just good-looking—it'll actually survive long enough for someone to fight over it at your estate sale someday.

Smoothing and Refining the Surface

Alright, let's take this basket-smoothing thing and crank it up a notch—because honestly, there's a whole world of little tricks and mindset shifts that separate an okay basket from the kind that makes people go, "Wait, you made this? For real?"

So, you've done the heavy lifting: coiling, stitching, cursing under your breath when a coil slipped, the whole shebang. But now, you're staring at this basket that's technically "done" but, let's be honest, still a little rough around the edges. Here's where you really get to flex your skills— think of it like the difference between a home haircut and a salon blowout. The basics are there, but the finishing touches? That's where the art lives.

First up, the inspection. Don't just spin the basket around in your hands and call it good. Get in there. Good lighting helps—a sunny window, a bright lamp, whatever. Maybe even run your hands over it with your eyes closed. Seriously. Your fingers will catch stuff your eyes miss. Raised spots, pokey bits, weird lumps—these are your targets. And yeah, it's a little tedious, but imagine if you spent hours weaving this thing just to have someone's sleeve catch on a stray bit of raffia. Nightmare.

Let's talk about those stray fibers and needle tips. Sometimes you'll find a pine needle sticking out like it's trying to escape. Instead of yanking it (which almost never ends well), grab whatever small, non-lethal pointy thing you've got. I've used hairpins, toothpicks—use what's handy. Tuck that escape artist back under the neighboring coils, and if you're feeling fancy, stitch it down with a bit of matching thread. Not only does it disappear, but you've just avoided future unravelling drama. And that's the name of the game: prevent headaches before they happen.

Loose threads? Oh, they love to sneak up on you. Snip them flush, but don't just toss the scissors after that. If you can, weave the end back in with a needle or even the tip of your scissors. It's a little extra effort, but dang, it makes the basket look seamless—like the fiber gods themselves wove it.

Now, pine needles and rattan are notorious for splitting. Sometimes you'll see a little crack or fray that makes the surface look janky. Don't freak out. Often, a gentle press with your thumb or a light trim does the trick, but always err on the side of caution. Better a tiny imperfection than weakening the whole structure. You're not chasing absolute perfection here (let's be real, nobody's gonna get that), but you do want it to feel good in the hand and look smooth to the eye.

Moisture—this is where things get almost spa-like for your basket. A light misting, not a downpour. I use an old spray bottle, but a damp washcloth works too. This step is pure gold, especially with natural fibers. It relaxes the whole thing, lets you kind of mold the shape, flatten out any weird bumps, and just generally coax the basket into its best self. Sometimes I'll even press the rim or bottom with my hands for a few minutes, or stack a couple of light books on top if I need everything to settle evenly.

But here's a hot tip: patience is your friend. Once it's damp and shaped up, walk away. Go watch an episode of something, read a book, whatever. Let it dry all the way. If you mess with it before it's completely dry, the coils might shift, or the shape could get weird again. Plus, letting the fibers "set" while drying means the basket holds its shape like a champ.

And honestly, this whole process is kinda meditative. You get to zone in, focus on all the little details, and end up with something that not only looks awesome but feels solid and professional. Over time, you'll develop your own tricks—maybe you'll discover a favorite tool for tucking or a secret recipe for a misting solution (a drop of lavender oil? Why not?). Every basket gets easier and more satisfying.

So, if you're really gunning for a super-smooth, pro-level finish—especially if your basket's got a wooden base or you've got some pesky needle tips sticking up at the rim—grab some ultra-fine sandpaper (think 220 up to 400 grit, nothing aggressive). Hit the rim with it, but honestly, go easy. You're not trying to take off layers, just knock down the rough spots or any little bits poking out. No need to go Hulk on it. Seriously, gentle is the way. If you overdo it, you might end up fraying the fibers, which is, uh, not great. This little sanding move really helps blend all the different materials together, so you get this seamless look. And here's a fun trick: after sanding, wrap the edge with something cool—maybe a thread in a wild color, or do a tight finishing coil. Suddenly your basket looks like it came straight out of a boutique, all smooth and polished, like you really knew what you were doing (which, you did).

How to Actually Keep Your Pine Needle Basket Looking Good

You spent all that time weaving, so don't blow it by treating your basket like just another dust-catcher. These things are tougher than they look (pine needles are no joke), but also weirdly sensitive to their environment—kind of like your houseplants, honestly.

Keep It Away from the Crazy Stuff

Let's talk sunlight first. Direct sun is basically a color vampire. Leave your basket baking in the window and those rich, golden pine needles will fade out to blah beige before you know it. Even your fancy threads or beads won't be safe. So, best move? Keep your basket somewhere bright, but away from the Death Star rays. And maybe give it a spin every once in a while so one side doesn't get all faded while the other stays fresh.

Then there's moisture—aka the silent destroyer. Too damp? You'll get mold and that funky, musty smell, and your basket will look like it's got chickenpox. Don't put it in the bathroom or next to that leaky basement wall. But don't go desert-dry, either. If things get too arid, the needles go brittle and snap, especially on the bends and ends. If you live somewhere super dry, maybe run a humidifier or even just leave a bowl of water out. Not rocket science—just try not to make your basket live in a sauna or a sand dune. Give it that "Goldilocks" treatment: not too hot, not too cold, not too wet, not too dry. That's how you keep it looking sweet for, like, decades.

Cleaning's not rocket science, but you do want to be gentle. Dust is the enemy, and it loves to sneak into all those nooks and crannies. Soft brush is your best friend here—think old makeup brush, soft artist's paintbrush, feather duster, whatever. Just give it a gentle sweep now and then so you don't end up with funky buildup. Don't get it wet, don't use weird cleaning sprays (trust me: disaster). Just treat it like you would a vintage record or a cat that hates baths—gentle and respectful.

Alright, let's get into the nitty gritty and spill a few extra basket secrets along the way.

So, when it comes to cleaning—look, everyone's first instinct is to go full power-wash mode, but pine needle baskets are a whole different beast. These things are basically the introverts of the basket world; they do NOT like attention in the form of water. Seriously, keep it to a cloth that's barely wet. If you wring it out and water still drips, you're doing it wrong. I've seen folks try to "freshen up" their baskets with a good soak and the regret is real. The structure goes all floppy, colors might run if there's any dye, and suddenly your lovely basket looks like it's survived a flood.

And don't even get me started on cleaning products. If you wouldn't use it on a baby, don't use it on your basket. Those natural fibers have oils and quirks, and harsh cleaners just strip the life right out of 'em. If you get a spot—grape juice, maybe, or some mysterious sticky goo (blame the kids)—grab a cotton swab or the corner of your barely-damp cloth, pat the area gently, and hope for the best. Always test in a spot no one will see, because nobody needs a random bleach mark front and center. Afterwards? Let it air dry naturally. No hair dryers, no sticking it by a heater—unless you're aiming for that "modern art" warped look.

Functional Use and Protective Linings

Now, let's talk about lining your basket. You'd be amazed at how a cheap bit of fabric can save your basket from an early grave. Felt, cotton, heck, even a clean old t-shirt cut to fit—anything soft that won't shed or bleed dye. The liner acts like a little shield, so if you're stashing apples, craft supplies, or your ever-growing key collection, you're not grinding grit and gunk directly into the pine needles. If you're a neat freak, you can even swap out the liner every week, and boom—your basket stays fresh with zero fuss. Liners also keep weird smells at bay, which, trust me, is a lifesaver if you ever forget about that orange at the bottom until it's… let's just say "past its prime."

Mindful Handling

And about handling—listen, you wouldn't pick up a fancy cake by the icing, right? Same logic. Always scoop from the bottom, supporting the weight like you care (because honestly, you should). The rim is there to look pretty and keep stuff from falling out, not to be a handle. If your basket's got handles, don't get cocky. They're for show, for light lifting—think a handful of mail, not a sack of potatoes. Overdo it and you'll hear that sad little snap that means you've just given your basket a new "feature"—aka, a broken handle.

One more thing: where you keep your basket matters. Shoving it into some damp corner or leaving it in the blazing sun will mess with the fibers. Pine needle baskets like the same conditions you do—dry, not too hot, not too cold, and definitely not humid. If you want your basket to live a long and happy life, keep it somewhere with a bit of airflow and no wild temperature swings.

Bottom line? Treat your basket like a treasured piece, not a disposable container. A little bit of care—gentle cleaning, smart lining, and respectful handling—means it'll still be looking way better than any plastic bin, years down the road. And let's be real, nothing says "I've got my life together" like a gorgeous, well-kept basket on the counter.

Long-Term Preservation and Display

So you've finished your basket and you're riding that high—seriously, nothing like seeing your own handiwork sitting pretty. But here's where most people zone out:

what happens next? I mean, you could just plop it on any old table and call it a day. But if you actually wanna keep it looking fresh (and, let's be honest, not like something you dug out of grandma's attic), you gotta think ahead.

Let's talk more about dust, because it's way sneakier than you'd think. You might not notice it at first, but give it a couple months and suddenly your basket's looking like it belongs in a haunted house. Dust isn't just gross—it actually grinds into those coils, wearing them down every time you brush it off. If you're serious about keeping your basket sharp, bust out a soft brush—think makeup brush, not your dad's old paintbrush—and gently sweep those nooks out every so often. Skip the canned air unless you wanna blow fibers loose and make a whole new mess.

Sunlight, though, is the silent killer. You might think, "Hey, natural light makes my basket look amazing." And it does… until it doesn't. Those UV rays don't mess around—they'll bleach colors out until your vibrant basket is rocking the same washed-out look as an old beach towel. If you're dead-set on putting a basket somewhere sunny, at least rotate it now and then so one side doesn't end up paler than the other. Or, better yet, invest in some curtains and keep those rays in check.

Now, about display cases—look, I know they sound a little museum-y, but hear me out. A good case actually saves you so much hassle. No more dusting every week, no surprise splashes from the kitchen, no greasy fingerprints from nosy relatives. And if you're worried about your basket being "locked away," remember, clear acrylic or glass keeps it totally visible. Plus, there's something that just feels right about giving your work that spotlight treatment. Like, "Yeah, I made that. It gets its own stage."

Let's get real about storage too. Not everyone's got the space to keep all their baskets on display 24/7. If you're tucking them away, use acid-free tissue or a

breathable cotton bag. Skip plastic bins—
that's pretty much inviting mold to the
party, especially if you live somewhere
humid. And don't stack them like
pancakes; a squashed basket is a sad
basket.

Oh, and displaying isn't just about what not
to do—it's a chance to get creative. Hang
baskets on the wall for some boho vibes,
or group them with other handmade stuff.
Mix in a plant or two, or prop them on
books. You don't have to treat your basket
like a precious artifact (unless you want
to), but showing it off in a way that fits your
style? That's the real flex.

Now, about the "patina" thing—people can
get weird about it. Some folks expect their
basket to look the same forever, like it's
made of plastic. But pine needles, cane,
willow—these are alive, or they were, and
they keep changing. Honestly, that's the
best part. Over time, those colors mellow
out, the gloss gets softer, and the whole
thing just feels richer, like a favorite old
leather jacket. When you give a basket as

a gift, don't just hand it over—tell its story. Explain how it'll age, why that's cool, and why a little change is a sign it's real, not some factory knockoff.

We should talk about repairs, too, because no matter how careful you are, stuff happens.

Maybe you nick it moving furniture, or your kid mistakes it for a hat. Don't panic. Most baskets are way tougher than they look, and half the time you can fix things yourself. If you've never done it, check out some videos or, even better, ask an experienced maker. There's a whole community out there that geeks out over this stuff—people love sharing tips, from the best thread to use to how to match a new pine needle to the old ones.
And honestly, those little repairs? They become part of the basket's story. Maybe you patch up a spot and add a bead or two—now it's got a memory attached. It's kinda like visible mending in clothes; instead of hiding the fix, you make it part of the design. Before you know it, you're not

just making baskets, you're preserving a little bit of yourself in every one.

Last thing: don't forget the emotional side. These baskets aren't just objects. They're hours of your life, your patience, your creativity all wrapped up in something you can actually touch. Every time you clean, move, or repair your basket, you're reconnecting with that process. It's weirdly grounding. And if you're lucky enough to pass a basket on—whether to a friend, a kid, or a total stranger—you're sending a piece of your story out into the world.

Long story short? Baskets aren't just for holding stuff. They hold memories, effort, and a kind of quiet pride. Take care of them, show them off, fix them up, and let them age. That's how they turn from "just a craft" into real, living art.

Let's just pause for a sec and really think about what's going on when you make one of these baskets. It's not like you're just weaving for the heck of it—every coil, every stubborn, pokey pine needle, it's all part of this weirdly intimate process. Kinda meditative, almost like you're zoning out to your own personal forest playlist. But also, you're sweating the small stuff: which needles are bendy enough, which ones snap, how much to soak 'em, how tight to pull the thread so you don't end up with a basket that's lopsided or, worse, unravels the first time someone sneezes near it.

And the story? It's not just your story. Those baskets are little time capsules. Like, imagine someone picking up your work decades from now and wondering who the heck had the patience to do all that. Maybe they'll catch a whiff of pine and be yanked back to some hike in the woods as a kid. It's wild how something as simple as a basket can drag all that history and nostalgia out of a person. Makes you realize—when you oil it, dust it, prop it up somewhere nice—it's not just about keeping it pretty. It's a legit act of respect. You're making sure the whispers from the forest, the rhythm of your hands, and all those hours hunched over your workbench don't just disappear into the ether.

Chapter 10: Advanced Projects and Techniques

Alright, so you've done your time in the pine needle trenches. Your first few baskets probably looked a little... let's say, "abstract." But now? You're crushing it. Your stitches are tight, your shapes look intentional, and you don't wince every time you jab your thumb. Congrats—welcome to the big leagues.

Now's when things actually get interesting. See, there's this whole world beyond the classic round or shallow basket. The real fun starts when you stop asking, "Can I make a basket?" and start asking, "What can't I make?" That's the advanced game. You start experimenting with stuff that's a little bonkers—think tall, dramatic cylinders that mess with gravity, vases with necks thinner than a pencil, boxes with lids so perfect they snap shut like a Tupperware, or wild, sculptural pieces that are basically pine needle modern art.

But here's the kicker: every new style comes with its own headaches. Tall shapes? Gravity will fight you. Make it too tight, it buckles. Too loose, it droops. Lidded containers? Good luck lining up those edges unless you're part robot. And when you start throwing curves or going for that "organic" look, suddenly your basket's got a mind of its own. This is the point where all those hours wrestling with beginner projects start to make sense. You need muscle memory, you need patience, and, honestly, you'll need a sense of humor because stuff will go sideways. That's part of the adventure.

But wait, there's more. Advanced basketry isn't just about wild shapes. It's about mixing and matching everything you know—like a chef going off-recipe. Maybe you start with a wood base (bonus points if you whittled it yourself). Maybe you're itching to try some hand-dyed threads you cooked up with onion skins and coffee grounds, or you go full magpie and stitch in shiny beads, shells, or even random stuff like old buttons or bits of leather. You're not just making a basket at this point. You're making a statement.

Of course, it's easy to get carried away. Pile on too many extras and, yeah, your basket's going to look like a Pinterest fail. There's an art to editing yourself, to knowing when to stop, and when to push just a little further. Some days, that means tearing out a whole section and starting over (not fun, but so worth it). Other times, it means embracing the weird, letting a "mistake" become the focal point. Honest truth? A lot of the best ideas come from happy accidents.

When you really get in the groove, something wild happens. Your techniques get fancier, sure, but your own style starts to shine through. You stop copying and start inventing. Maybe you gravitate to earthy, raw finishes. Maybe you love high-contrast colors and bold, geometric patterns. Or maybe you're into subtle, textural stuff that rewards people who look close. Whatever it is, the basket's not just a basket—it's your basket. It tells a story, not just about pine needles and thread, but about you. And every time you push a little further, try a new shape, or mess around with a new technique, you're expanding what this craft can be. Plus, let's be real— there's nothing better than someone picking up your work and saying, "Wait, you made this?" That's the good stuff.

So, don't be afraid to screw up. Don't be afraid to go big, or weird, or totally off-script. The best part about advanced basketry is that it's basically an endless playground. The more you play, the more you learn, and the more your own voice comes through in every single coil.

Alright, let's go deeper. I mean, basketry's a rabbit hole, right? You start out just wanting a cute thing to toss your spare change in, and before you know it, you're plotting out blueprints for the ultimate utensil holder that'll make your kitchen look like Martha Stewart moved in.

Let's talk about those "advanced projects" for a minute—because, honestly, that's where the magic happens. When you get specific with your designs, it's not just about showing off. You're actually solving real-life headaches, like the endless tangle of pens or the existential crisis. These baskets start to feel like little life hacks you handcrafted yourself. And the beauty is, every time you design something tailored—a tall, skinny basket for spatulas, a low, flat tray for your collection of travel souvenirs—you're learning how the function shapes the form. It's like, the more you think about what the basket needs to do, the more creative you get with how it looks. And sometimes you end up with something you didn't even plan, but it works better than anything you could've bought at the store. Plus, let's be real, it's ten times more satisfying to say, "Yeah, I made that."

Now, lidded baskets? Total game-changers. Not only do they stash your stuff away, but they're also little treasure chests—half the fun is opening them up.

And if you figure out how to add compartments or dividers? You're not just making a basket; you're engineering a storage solution. It's like Tupperware got classy. I've seen people do crazy things with these, like hidden layers or secret pockets. Makes you feel like a wizard, honestly.

The multi-compartment organizers? Next-level. If you're into crafts, or you've got kids with all those tiny Lego bits, making something that actually fits your stuff (instead of cramming it into a generic bin) is a total power move. And when you nail it, your friends will be asking you to make them one—trust me.

Let's talk stitches—because once you've got the basic coil down, things get spicy. You start playing with advanced stitches and suddenly your basket's not just holding snacks, it's got a personality. I'm talking texture you want to run your hands over, patterns that actually make you stop and stare for a second. You might mess up the first few times, but honestly, that's part of the fun. You learn more from a crooked stitch than a perfect one.

The diagonal stitch is such a small tweak, but it changes everything. It's like putting a twist on a classic recipe—suddenly, there's depth, movement, and it just feels more alive. Plus, it does double-duty by making the basket sturdier. Nothing worse than spending hours making something that flops over as soon as you put anything in it. The diagonal stitch's got your back.

Then there's the triple wrap stitch. If you want drama, this is it. It makes the edges pop, gives the basket some weight—like, you can actually feel the difference. It's perfect for when you want to highlight a certain part, or just flex your skills a bit. And the best part is, you can mix and match these stitches. Do a row of triple wraps, then switch to a diagonal, then maybe throw in something totally weird you made up on the fly. Who's gonna stop you? There are no rules—just what looks and feels right for you.

Honestly, what I love about this whole thing is how personal it gets. Every decision, from the shape to the stitches, is yours. And the more you experiment, the more you start to trust your own instincts. Sometimes you think you've messed something up, but then you realize it's actually kind of genius. That's what makes it art, not just craft.

So yeah, advanced basketry isn't just about "better baskets." It's about inventing, problem-solving, and making stuff that means something—to you, and probably to the people who end up fighting over your baskets at family gatherings. It's hands-on therapy, a creative outlet, and a practical skill all rolled into one. And honestly, once you get a taste of that kind of accomplishment, you'll never look at a store-bought basket the same way again.

So, picture this: you're sitting there with a pile of pine needles, maybe a cup of tea, maybe something stronger (no judgment), and suddenly you realize—this isn't just about making a basket to hold your keys.

You're basically channeling nature and your own weird, wonderful ideas through your hands. Stitch length? Totally up to you. You wanna go long and loose for a wave vibe, or short and tight for that zigzag chevron look? Go nuts. Change direction mid-stitch, and suddenly the basket's got this flow, like it's moving even when it's just sitting there. Seriously, it's wild how much personality you can squeeze out of a bunch of dried needles and some thread.

And don't even get me started on color. There's a whole universe there. Maybe you start out with a nice earthy brown, then fade into a mossy green, and finish off with a little pop of indigo just because you felt like it. It's not just pretty for pretty's sake—it actually guides the way people look at your work, like invisible arrows pointing to the best bits. Oh, and if you stumble on some natural dyes or, I don't know, decide to raid your backyard for materials, suddenly your basket isn't just handmade, it's hyper-local, almost like a map of where you've been and what you've seen. It's honestly kind of poetic.

But, okay, real talk: don't expect to nail it on your first try. I mean, unless you're some kind of basket savant, you're gonna mess up. And that's fine. It's actually the best part. Take a chunk of leftover material—or even just start a mini basket—so you can screw around without the fear of ruining hours of work. Tension too tight? Loosen up. Angle looks weird? Try again. You'll screw up, you'll laugh (or swear), but every mistake is just another step to getting better. Eventually you stop thinking about the "right" way to do it and just… do it. Your style starts showing up, and suddenly, it's like the basket is telling your story. At that point, you're not just following a tutorial. You're straight-up making art.

Combining Materials and Mixed Media

Now, about throwing in other materials—this is where things get spicy. Wood is a classic for good reason. It's sturdy, it's beautiful, and it plays so well with the rougher texture of pine needles. Plus, you get to carve stuff or leave it all rustic and natural, depending on your mood. Then there's fabric. Want to go vintage grandma-chic? Line it with floral cotton. Feeling fancy? Silk. That fabric lining isn't just for show—it keeps your basket's contents from poking through and adds a whole new layer of color and softness. It's like turning your basket into a little treasure chest.

Metal is a curveball, but used right, it's a total game-changer. Weave in a thin copper wire for a glint of shine, or go bold with a metal rim or some geometric accents. Suddenly your basket is less "country market" and more "art gallery opening." And if you want to get really traditional (or just love a good texture mash-up), add in other natural fibers.

Raffia, sweetgrass, jute—each one brings its own feel and strength. The basket gets tougher, more interesting, and people will literally want to touch it just to see what's going on.

And for the love of all things crafty, don't skimp on the handles. Leather braids? So comfy and they last forever. Wood handles? All about that earthy, grounded vibe. And hey, if you want to get extra, use antlers, beads, or even old jewelry. Why not? The handle is the handshake of the basket—it's the first thing people touch, so make it count.

Honestly, this whole process is about more than just winding stuff into a container. It's about experimenting, finding that sweet spot between chaos and control, and making something that's as useful as it is beautiful. Every basket you make is a snapshot of where you are right now— skill-wise, mood-wise, life-wise. And trust me, people can tell. That's what makes it art, not just craft. So go ahead, mix it up, mess around, and don't be afraid to make something weird. That's where the magic happens.

So, beads, shells, stones—those aren't just for show. They're like the tattoos of the basket world. Every time you stitch one of those suckers in, you're dropping a little hint about who you are or where you've been. Picture it: you're out hiking, you find this odd-shaped pebble, and next thing you know, it's riding shotgun in your next project. That's not just art; that's a time capsule. You could even say it's a low-key brag—"Yeah, I hiked there, and I made this."

And let's not skip over the color game. Dying pine needles? That's next-level wizardry. People are out here boiling up onion skins or raiding the craft store for the brightest dyes, just so their baskets can pop. You ever seen a basket with that perfect ombre fade, shifting from deep forest green to a sun-bleached yellow? That's not an accident. That's hours of mixing, testing, cursing, and maybe a little bit of luck. There's this whole underground world of pine needle dye recipes—some folks guard them like family secrets. And it's not just about looking pretty; it's about mood, about telling a story with color the same way a painter does.

Now, once you start blending in all these materials, it's not just "throw it together and hope for the best." Nah, it's more like solving a 3D puzzle, except if you mess up, your basket might sag or snap. You've got to figure out if that shell's too heavy for the side, or if those glass beads will cut through your thread. It's basically basketry meets engineering. I mean, who knew you'd need to think about tensile strength or weight distribution when you started out just wanting to make something pretty for your coffee table?

And here's a little secret: even seasoned basket makers have horror stories. Stuff like, "I spent two weeks dying needles, then the color bled everywhere the second I got it wet," or "I stitched in this gorgeous agate, and it cracked my entire coil." It's all part of the process—frustrating as heck, but honestly, sometimes those "mistakes" turn into the coolest design features. You gotta roll with it. Sometimes your basket wants to be something different than you planned, and you just have to let it.

But—and this is key—no matter how much you want to go wild with the decorations, if you don't have those coils tight and your stitches locked in, the whole thing's a lost cause. It's like building a house with glitter glue instead of nails. Every experienced maker knows: keep those basics solid, or you're just making a fancy pile of pine needles. All the shiny stuff is just icing on the cake.

At the end of the day, this whole mixed media thing is about pushing limits— seeing how far you can stretch tradition without snapping it. The best baskets? They're mashups: old-school skill meets new-school vibe. They tell stories, hold memories, and yeah, sometimes they even make you laugh when you remember all the trial-and-error disasters along the way. That's the magic. It's not just a craft;

it's a living, evolving thing—and every new basket's a chance to try something you've never done before.

Mastering Large and Sculptural Forms

Alright, let's really get into the weeds here—because, honestly, making big, show-stopping pine needle baskets is a whole different beast than the "cute little bowl for mom" routine. You're basically jumping off the deep end and hoping you can swim. Or at least float.

First thing: prep work. People think you just grab a handful of needles and start spiraling away, but that's like thinking you can just pick up a guitar and instantly shred like Hendrix. Nope. You need to obsess over your materials. We're talking sifting through bags of pine needles, tossing the brittle ones, lining up the longest, most flexible sticks like you're about to build a tiny log cabin. And don't even get me started on soaking them. If you don't get the moisture just right, those needles will snap on you mid-coil and you'll want to throw the whole project out the window. Seriously, it's more spa day than craft hour.

And then—coils. Do you go fat, heavy-duty ropes for a basket that could probably survive a hurricane, or do you risk going skinny for those delicate, mind-bending details? There's no right answer. It's all about trade-offs. The thicker the coil, the sturdier and more dramatic your piece, but good luck wrangling that monster into a tight curve. Go thin and you'll get killer detail, but don't cry when it starts to sag under its own weight. It's like choosing between hiking boots and ballet slippers— you gotta know where you're going.

Let's talk about vision. Sculptural baskets aren't just pretty storage. They're conversation starters, statement pieces, sometimes even a little bit of visual chaos. You could make a basket that looks like a tidal wave or a dragon, or one that's so lopsided and unpredictable that people have to ask, "Wait, what is that supposed to be?" And honestly, that's half the fun.

The whole point is to push boundaries—yours, and the craft's. There's a reason you don't see these things at every farmer's market.

Now, the real grind: construction. No one tells you how heavy a big basket gets by the time you're halfway done. Forget sitting cross-legged on the floor. You'll be propping this beast up on your knees, the table, your cat—whatever keeps it from sagging while you stitch. And don't even try to finish it all in one go unless you hate your wrists. Chopping it up into sections is the only way to keep your sanity. Each coil is its own battle—get it right, then move on. It's like building a house brick by brick, but way less predictable.

Here's another thing: support tools are your best friends. I'm talking balloons, sandbags, weird wooden forms your neighbor side-eyes you for making in the garage. Sometimes you gotta MacGyver the heck out of it just to keep the shape you want. The bigger you go, the more gravity tries to ruin your day. A tiny mistake on a small basket? No biggie. On a giant one, it's like dropping a paint can on your canvas halfway through a masterpiece.

And the shaping—oh, the shaping. If you want curves, windows, or wild angles, you're basically wrestling with the thing. Sometimes you start with one idea and halfway through you realize you've created a mutant. You gotta roll with it. Maybe you need to sneak in a bit of wire for backup or suddenly change your whole stitch pattern because that curve you wanted is now looking more like a potato chip than a wave. It's all improvisation, and it's messy, and sometimes you're just crossing your fingers that it holds together until the last stitch.

You know what? That's where the magic happens. Every sculptural basket is a lesson in stubbornness and patience. You'll mess up. You'll get frustrated. You'll wonder why you didn't just take up knitting. But every time you finish, you've learned something—about balance, about how much you can push the materials (and yourself), and about being okay with things not going exactly to plan. It's like each basket is a little bootcamp for your creative brain.

On top of all that, there's the buzz of experimenting. Maybe you start mixing in other stuff—yarns, beads, random wire, even scraps from other failed projects. Pine needle basketry suddenly isn't just about tradition; it's about seeing how far you can stretch an old technique into something totally fresh. The more you push, the more you realize there aren't any real rules—just a bunch of guidelines that are begging to be broken.

So, yeah, if you're thinking about going big and bold with pine needles, don't stress about perfection. Embrace the weirdness. Make mistakes. Make something that makes you laugh or groan or both. Worst-case scenario? You've got a lopsided art piece and a killer story. Best case? You blow your own mind—and maybe everyone else's, too.

I hope that you enjoyed reading through this book and that you have found it useful. If you want to share your thoughts on this book, you can do so by leaving a review On the Amazon page. Have a great rest of the day.

Printed in Dunstable, United Kingdom

71800118R00100